Living Without
PROCRASTINATION

M. Susan Roberts, Ph.D.

MJF Books
New York

Published by MJF Books
Fine Communications
Two Lincoln Square
60 West 66th Street
New York, NY 10023

Living Without Procrastination
LC Control Number 99-070056
ISBN 1-56731-307-8

This edition published by arrangement with New Harbinger Publications, Inc.

Manufactured in the United States of America on acid-free paper ∞

MJF Books and the MJF colophon are trademarks of Fine Creative Media, Inc.

BG   10 9 8 7 6 5 4 3 2 1

Contents

Acknowledgments

I want to thank Dr. George Semb of the University of Kansas who gave me my first opportunity to work with students on their problems with procrastination. I also want to thank Dr. Quentin Regestein of Brigham and Women's Hospital, in Boston, for encouraging me in my research and writing on the topic of procrastination. I am especially grateful to my husband, Dr. Gerard Jansen, who convinced me that I should write this book and who contributed significantly to its content.

Preface

In the last twenty years there has been an increase in the research and treatment of procrastination. My own interest began while student teaching at the University of Kansas. The introductory developmental psychology course that I taught used a self-paced teaching format. Students studied at their own pace and then took tests when they were ready. They were required to work on material until they mastered it. The self-paced system has been demonstrated to be an effective teaching method and students like it. The problem came at the end of every semester when students attempted to complete the majority of course work in the last three weeks. It was a discouraging experience for students and faculty. My colleagues and I began to investigate procrastination among students in our classrooms. We were specifically looking at ways to motivate students and to teach them to plan their work. We found methods that effectively increased student awareness of deadlines. We arranged for peers to work together and to provide feedback to each other throughout the semester. Students also learned to plan and to consider tasks in relationship to other demands in their lives. We found that using this system students were able to finish the course well before the semester deadline. The techniques of planning and monitoring apply to many procrastination tasks and will be discussed throughout this book.

After finishing school I continued my concern with the understanding and treatment of procrastination. For several years I taught a course at a local adult education center for adults who were struggling to overcome this problem. The participants provided great support for one another and discovered a lot of new ideas for getting things done. The format I used in leading these groups is the basis for the organization of this book.

The renewed interest in procrastination largely has been concerned with the problem of academic underachievement. A goal of the educational system is to produce highly skilled individuals who can find satisfying, productive employment. When motivation lapses and students cannot study effectively or complete their programs, the educational mission is jeopardized. Solutions to the specific problem of procrastination play an important role in improving student performance and in the success of the educational system. Underachievement is costly not only in personal terms but also in reduced contribution to society.

Procrastination also has serious implications for our personal health and the costs of health care. A 1990 study by Carol Schechter, Corinne Vanchieri, and Christine Crofton cites procrastination as a leading reason for women not receiving regular mammograms. The authors report that breast cancer is a leading cause of cancer-related deaths in women and may be reduced as much as 30 percent if regular mammograms are obtained. Other studies link procrastination to medical problems such as the diagnosis and treatment of prostate cancer, high cholesterol, and AIDS. Most medical problems can be treated successfully and more simply if they are detected early. The expense in terms of human suffering and more radical treatments can be linked to problems with procrastination. Clearly, we need to be concerned about procrastination and its cost to all of us.

This book was written with the hope of reducing the frustration and loss that results from unwanted procrastination. The book is not written to be an inspirational message that fades shortly after reading. Rather, it is written as a practical manual for change. It provides a step-by-step method for ending procrastination. Change may not occur quickly and it does take effort. But, as students have shown me over the years and in many settings, it can occur.

1

Introduction

Ben just canceled his dental appointment for the second time this year. He is aware of the importance of preventative medicine but feels he is just too busy right now. He is, after all, working eleven hours a day on a project for the office. It's a week until the deadline and he can feel the panic mounting. Ben has difficulty estimating how long a job will take. He is also pretty disorganized—he often misplaces key documents and spends a lot of time looking for things.

Ben has struggled with procrastination for as long as he can remember. He postpones so many activities of life that he has a hard time remembering what excuse he used with each friend or co-worker. Over the years teachers, parents, and friends have tried to help. They can't understand why Ben chooses to live with so much worry and dread about not getting things done. Ben has lived this way for so long he can only rarely imagine another way to think and feel about what he has to do. Ben is frustrated and angry about his inability to get started and to finish a task. He wonders if there is something wrong with his character or if he's just lazy.

Ben shares a number of common characteristics with those who procrastinate. He is disorganized, has difficulty estimating the time that work will take, and feels down about his behavior and himself. He often feels overwhelmed and doesn't know where to start. As repeated attempts to improve his performance fail, he begins to blame himself—or his bad character—for his problem.

Ben's problem with procrastination is pervasive. He avoids situations at home, work, and even in his social life. Others have problems with procrastination that are more situationally specific. Marge, for example, had little trouble completing high school. She was generally very organized and could get her schoolwork done and still have time for drama club and bike racing. Marge is less sure of herself now that she has started college. She is doing fine in history and science, but English composition is difficult. Marge is having real trouble completing the monthly papers required in the course. Marge worries about picking a great topic and then spends days wondering how to make the paper exceptional. She often stares at a blank page for hours. Marge's self-confidence is slipping. She wonders about her ability to write and even to make it in college. Initially she blamed others for her situation. She felt her high school had been a poor one and that her teachers had not adequately prepared her for the work she now faces. Then Marge began to realize that she can control the present. She began to work on controlling her anxiety and signed up for some tutorials on writing papers.

Both Ben and Marge have a significant problem with procrastination. For Ben, avoidance is a way of life. Marge's problem is situation specific. Researchers are now calling Ben's lifestyle of avoidance *trait procrastination*. It is so pervasive that it can be considered a personal trait. It will characterize his behavior in almost any situation. Marge exhibits *state procrastination*. Procrastination is not typical of Marge but does create a problem for her from time to time. Joseph Ferrari and his colleagues refer to this type of procrastination as "atypical." Many people such as Marge are productive in most situations of life but occasionally find it extremely difficult to start or to finish one project or one type of task. There is, however, a continuum between engaging in chronic procrastination and avoiding just one situation. Most people fall somewhere in the middle.

Definition of Procrastination

The word *procrastination* comes from a Latin verb *procrastinare*, meaning to put off until tomorrow. Over the centuries it has been referred to as sin or sloth, reflecting a real concern with unnecessary delay. Survival can, of course, depend on getting things done, such as keeping tools repaired and crops harvested. This concern with procrastination is reflected in the folklore and proverbs of many cultures. Consider our own sayings, "Don't put off until tomorrow what you can do today" or "A stitch in time saves nine." Other proverbs include the English saying, "One of these days is none of these days" and the Italian, "Between saying and doing many a pair of shoes is worn out." Literature too contains some colorful expressions, such as Edward Young's 1742 line, "Procrastination is the thief of time."

Procrastination has been thought of as a simple problem of time management, but efforts to reduce procrastination with improved time management techniques have not been effective. As you will see later, procrastination has emotional and cognitive components in addition to organizational and time management dimensions. It is also important to distinguish procrastination from indecision. Procrastination occurs when a person makes a decision but does not follow through. It is possible to procrastinate on making decisions, but this type of procrastination is not seen as different from any other postponed task.

Procrastination is a complex behavior made up of thinking, feeling, and behavioral components. Clarry Lay, a professor of psychology, defines procrastination as "the tendency to postpone that which is necessary to reach some goal." Goals are personal, and what seems like a goal to one person (for example, getting a job or maintaining good health) is not necessarily a priority for someone else. But when a task has value to you and your behavior does not follow, procrastination is occurring. It may be hard to see some everyday tasks as goals. Doing the laundry, for example, may not seem meaningful. But doing the laundry is a subtask or subgoal toward the real goal of keeping the house running smoothly so that other important activities can occur. Procrastination also occurs when smaller steps toward larger goals are not taken.

Procrastination also involves feelings. Albert Ellis and William Knaus, psychologists, define procrastination as "delaying task completion to the point of experiencing subjective discomfort." The discomfort may come from a variety of emotions such as anxiety, guilt, or dread. Discomfort often is experienced at the moment action is postponed. It is terminated by turning to easier, more pleasurable distractions. However, the discomfort returns as days (or hours) pass and additional decisions to delay are made. Discomfort builds until it is intolerable and something is done to relieve it. Some people do not experience discomfort about not getting things done. These are optimistic people who feel that they can procrastinate and still have things turn out well. The experience of discomfort comes after the deadline is missed and the consequence is paid—such as late fees, a car that breaks down on the road, and so on.

The third component of procrastination is the irrational nature of the act. Lay also defines procrastination as the "irrational tendency to delay tasks that should be completed." Irrational in this sense does not mean crazy but rather the lack of a reason for delay. Procrastination occurs when there is no real impediment to action, for example, incapacity or illness, famine or flood. In other words, behavior could occur but it does not. Irrational also refers to the senseless harm that is done to the self by putting off something that would be of benefit. Procrastination involves choosing smaller, short-term rewards over larger, long-term rewards. This choice is ultimately self-defeating. It is irrational not to try to change.

Procrastination occurs when a goal—meaningful behavior—is delayed for no necessary reason and discomfort results. It is difficult to assess procrastination for someone else. You are the best judge of your goals, discomfort at not pursuing them, and what really stands in your way.

Procrastination Survey

Clarry Lay has studied procrastination for many years and has developed a questionnaire to assess problems with procrastination in adults. The survey is used extensively in research and has been shown to be reliable and valid. It also is being used in cross-cultural studies. It is reproduced on the following pages for you to rate your own level of procrastination.

Frequency of Procrastination

If you score above average on the Lay questionnaire, you are not alone. In a 1989 survey of adults by William McGown and Judith

Johnson, 25 percent reported that procrastination was an important problem for them. Even more, 40 percent, reported that procrastination cost them money in the past year. Other studies of adults in the workplace also indicate that procrastination is a significant problem in their lives.

A survey of college students by M.B. Hill and colleagues found that 27 percent reported always or frequently procrastinating. A substantial number of the students, 23 percent, reported procrastinating about half of the time. Taken together, that is 50 percent of the students who felt they procrastinated most of the time! G. Beswick and colleagues found similar results among Australian students. Forty-six percent reported nearly always or always procrastinating and 62 percent of students wanted to do something about it. Procrastination should not be underestimated. It is a frequent and difficult problem that is causing much suffering for many.

How to Use This Book

This book provides you with a complete manual for change. It emphasizes doing, thinking, and behaving differently toward your task than you have in the past. The introductory chapters review the current knowledge of procrastination. But the book is not really theoretical. It is intended to help you to understand the problem of procrastination and then to do something about it.

Lack of planning is common among those who procrastinate. Very often, people who delay do not systematically follow an overall plan for getting things done. This book is designed to provide you with a complete plan of action. Use the Task Work Sheet at the end of this chapter as your overall planning guide. You will complete sections of the work sheet as you read and work through material in the following chapters. Overcoming procrastination will get easier as you plan your approach to each task you encounter. I recommend that you photocopy the work sheet and use it for future tasks. The plan you develop will not only address issues of managing time (although they are included) but will also consider how you think and feel about your task.

Self-help books are meant to assist you in clarifying your problem and taking action to solve it. This book, though, is not intended

Exercise

For each of the twenty questions, circle either true or false as it applies to your behavior now. If you have trouble choosing either true or false, pick the one that best fits your most recent experience.

1. I often find myself performing tasks that I had intended   T   F
   to do days before.

2. I often miss concerts, sporting events, or the like,   T   F
   because I don't get around to buying the tickets on time.

3. When planning a party, I make the necessary   T   F
   arrangements well in advance.

4. When it is time to get up in the morning, I most often   T   F
   get right out of bed.

5. A letter may sit for days after I write it before mailing it.   T   F

6. I generally return phone calls promptly.   T   F

7. Even with jobs that require little else except sitting   T   F
   down and doing them, I find they often don't get
   done for days.

8. I usually make decisions as soon as possible.   T   F

9. I generally delay before starting on work I have to do.   T   F

10. When traveling, I usually have to rush in preparing to   T   F
    arrive at the airport or station at the appropriate time.

11. When preparing to go out, I am seldom caught having   T   F
    to do something at the last minute.

12. In preparing for some deadline, I often waste time by   T   F
    doing other things.

13. If a bill for a small amount comes, I pay it right away.   T   F

14. I usually return an R.S.V.P. request very shortly after   T   F
    receiving the invitation.

15. I often have a task finished sooner than necessary.   T   F

16. I always seem to end up shopping for birthday or   T   F
    Christmas gifts at the last minute.

17. I usually buy even an essential item at the last minute.   T   F

18. I usually accomplish all the things I plan to do in a day.   T   F

19. I am continually saying "I'll do it tomorrow."   T   F

20. I usually take care of all the tasks I have to do before   T   F
I settle down and relax for the evening.

To score the questionnaire, give yourself one point each for questions 1, 2, 5, 7, 9, 10, 12, 16, 17, and 19 that you answered true. Give yourself one point each for questions 3, 4, 6, 8, 11, 13, 14, 15, 18, and 20 that you answered false. Total the points for true and false items. If your total score is 9 or greater, you are above average in your tendency to procrastinate. If your score is 13 or above, you are experiencing an extreme degree of difficulty with procrastination.

for people who have life-threatening issues that also involve procrastination. If you are engaging in dangerous or risky behavior and want to stop, or if your problems with procrastination have worsened over time, you should consult a professional. Recent research by McGown and Roberts links procrastination to substance abuse and post-traumatic stress disorder. The relationship of procrastination and depression and anxiety has been well known for years. If you have other significant clinical problems, you should not attempt to solve them alone. This book could be an excellent adjunct to therapy for any of these serious clinical problems.

The program outlined in this book is one that I developed from leading groups on overcoming procrastination. Over the course of several years, hundreds of students have used the program. Some students were able to solve lifelong goals, such as applying and being accepted to law school; others worked on smaller, day-to-day tasks they had been avoiding.

To make the program work for you, you must be active. Most chapters include exercises designed to get you involved in the material. They ask you to try out a new idea or to assess your current situation. It is important to complete each of the exercises by writing out your answers. If you find that you are skipping the exercises or just mentally answering the questions, you are not serious about change. You may be dabbling intellectually but not really making a commitment. To move beyond this stage, you need to clarify your reasons for completing your task (read Chapter 6 on task-directed thinking). Then go back to the beginning and start the program again—this time with active participation.

It is important that you read the book all the way through. The first chapters will help you to diagnose your style of procrastination and to be better prepared to catch yourself in temporary slips. The action-oriented chapters will be the basis for your plan for accomplishment. You can peruse or skip the chapters on school, work, or leisure if they do not immediately relate to your current situation. You will benefit from reading these chapters at a later time or when you select your next task to complete.

Selecting a Task

To begin, select one task to focus on throughout this book. This task will be your sounding board for all the ideas that follow. You should apply every concept and technique to this task. Continually ask yourself questions about the material, such as How does that idea apply to me? or How will I apply that technique to my task? This questioning approach will increase your participation and benefits.

When working with people who procrastinate, I encourage them to choose a small problem to work on. The problem should be something of value to you but not of momentous proportions—a practice problem. You will need to focus your energy on the change process and less on the task itself. You may be able to think of a dozen such problems. You can list any number of jobs around the house or office that you have been avoiding. If a simple task does not come readily to mind, consider the following categories of everyday life and select one that has been a problem for you.

Social
writing letters
planning a party
returning phone calls
buying presents
returning R.S.V.P.
inviting friends over to
    your house
visiting friends/family

Work
arriving on time
filing
completing reports
answering mail/phone calls
planning a meeting
asking for a raise

School
writing papers
studying
choosing a major/dissertation
    topic
making appointment with
    a professor
returning library books

Leisure
going out to movies, concerts
learning a relaxation technique
joining a gym
going to the gym
exercising regularly
learning a new hobby

Health
making doctor appointments
taking prescribed medication
reading on topic of concern
eating healthy diet
getting routine tests
evaluating eyeglasses
quitting smoking or other habit

Financial
balancing checkbook
paying bills
planning for the future
checking on credit rating
saving
making a will

Home
making routine repairs
routine cleaning
buying furniture
planning remodeling
mowing the lawn
installing new equipment
discarding items
organizing space
routine maintenance

Personal Care
buying new clothes
doing laundry
personal hygiene
getting a haircut
mending clothes
keeping nails clean/cut
brushing/flossing teeth

Once you have selected the task you will work on throughout this book, you are ready to set a goal.

Setting a Goal

The next step is to make your task measurable. Some tasks sound great at the outset but on further inspection seem vague, making direct action difficult. For example, you may have chosen to return phone calls as your focus. But you may start to wonder, which phone calls? all phone calls? how soon? Without specifying who, how many, where, and when, you continue to leave yourself open to procrastination. Without clear expectations, it will still be easy to say, "Well, I'm tired now. I'll call tomorrow."

For the task you are to work on throughout this book—and for any task you seriously want to complete—you must spell out the specifics. Then you are able to honestly evaluate your effort and hold yourself accountable. By specifying, "I will return all sales calls within twelve working hours," your goal is very clear. Either you make all the calls or you don't.

The exercise below will help you clarify the task you selected for yourself. Rewrite the task with the specifics of who, what, when, where, and how much. Then turn to the Task Work Sheet and transfer the clarified goal to the work sheet. Keep the work sheet available. You will use it throughout this book. Your program will build as you read until your work sheet provides a complete action plan to achieve your goal.

Exercise

Evaluate the following examples for the specifics of who, what, when, where, and how many:

1. Vague: I'm going to start getting to work on time.
   Clear: I'll be at my desk by 7:55 a.m.

2. Vague: I'm going to start saving for a new car.
   Clear: I'll save $50 every pay period starting next Friday.

3. Vague: I want to quit smoking.
   Clear: I will sign up for a smoking cessation program at the health center by Thursday.

4. Vague: I'm going to stop wearing socks with holes in them.
   Clear: I'm going to buy six pairs of socks this Saturday.

Task Work Sheet

Date:

1. Task: _____

   _____

   _____

2. Estimated time to complete: _____

3. Deadline for completion: _____

4. Excuses I have used for not getting it done: _____

   _____

   _____

   _____

5. Techniques I will use to complete the task: _____

   _____

   _____

   _____

6. Benefits I will get from completing the task: _____

   _____

   _____

7. Relaxation techniques I will use: _____

   _____

   _____

8. Support techniques I will use: _____

   _____

   _____

9. Review/revision date: _____

2

Procrastination Traits

Recent research on procrastination provides insight into the characteristics of those who put off and delay work. A number of traits are emerging and can be found consistently across studies. The growing body of information may finally put to rest the simplistic, stereotypical notions about procrastination. People who procrastinate are complex individuals with diverse motivations for their postponement of tasks. They experience a variety of emotions, engage in different patterns of avoidance, and possess a range of personality traits.

There are two distinct profiles of those who procrastinate. One type is characterized by overarousal. This person constantly attends to the environment, becomes overwhelmed, and may avoid work as a way of coping. A second type of procrastination is marked by underarousal. In this case, the person has difficulty maintaining attention, so projects are not started or are left undone. It is possible to have some or all of the traits of both types of procrastination. In the real world, pure types rarely exist. This chapter outlines current knowledge about procrastination and its traits.

Procrastination and Gender

Procrastination occurs as frequently for men as for women. No studies to date have found a difference by gender in the frequency or severity of procrastination. Most characteristics of those who procrastinate also occur equally for both sexes. Both anxiety and depression, for example, are associated with procrastination and occur as frequently for women as for men. Also, test anxiety has been shown to occur at equal rates for both sexes. In an assessment of life adjustment for people who procrastinate, Norman Milgram did find one gender difference: men who procrastinate report less satisfaction with life than do women.

Procrastination and Age

A 1994 study of people ranging in age from eighteen to seventy-seven by McGown and Roberts found a relationship between age and gender for those who procrastinate. The authors found that for men, procrastination peaks in the middle-to-late twenties. Problems then decline over the next forty years but increase around age sixty. Women showed a somewhat similar pattern. For women, procrastination peaks at about twenty-five. Procrastination declines until age fifty-five and then increases. The increase in procrastination for women in later years is greater than it is for men. Since the McGown and Roberts survey was the first to look at procrastination along the spectrum of age, it is not possible to say whether these results will hold up over time. It may be that future generations will have the benefit of learning to combat procrastination at an early age and not need to endure the problem into adulthood.

Studies of college students by Hill and colleagues found that procrastination increases, rather than decreases, over the years. Students' reported problems with delay increased in each of the freshman, sophomore, junior, and senior years. There is some suggestion that students older than the typical college age do procrastinate less when they return to school.

There does not seem to be any relationship between procrastination and birth order. Ferrari and his colleague M. J. Olivette studied adolescent girls who procrastinated in making decisions.

They found no differences in reports of procrastination for girls born first, second, or third in the family. In larger families, girls who were among the older, middle, or younger groups of siblings also did not differ in their tendency to procrastinate.

Procrastination and Intelligence

People who procrastinate often put themselves down by calling themselves stupid or lazy. But so far, no study has suggested that procrastinators are less intelligent than others. In a 1979 study, using a standard intelligence test, R. Taylor found no differences in IQs of people who procrastinate and those who do not. Later, Ferrari looked at verbal intelligence (vocabulary and information) and abstract intelligence and found no differences among those who procrastinate and those who don't.

Some authors suggest that students who have higher ability in a subject are *more* likely to procrastinate. The assumption is that students who are good at a subject feel less pressure to get the work done, knowing that they can succeed with a last-minute effort. At present there is little information to confirm or deny this hypothesis. However, McGown and Ferrari did show that students who procrastinate perform less well and retain less than students who do not.

Overarousal and Procrastination

Many people who procrastinate report feeling overwhelmed a lot of the time. They seem to be always thinking and attending to what is going on around them. They have difficulty tuning out unnecessary stimulation and settling down to do a job. Anxiety is a common experience, including worry about how their performance will be judged by others. Procrastination results as a way of coping with fear. People who are overaroused find it extremely difficult to calm themselves down and return to a state of equilibrium. By putting off the task, they avoid the negative arousal that goes with it.

Wilma is forty-five years old, single, and working as a legal secretary at a large corporate law firm in Boston. She sought help for anxiety and procrastination at a local clinic. An initial interview ruled out issues of trauma, abuse, and alcohol or drugs. Wilma reported that her childhood had been unremarkable except that her family relocated from the Midwest when she was eight years old. Wilma felt generally anxious. Her mind was always going and she had a hard time settling down to sleep at night. She worried a lot and reviewed her every performance critically. She felt the disapproval of others even before any comments were made.

Further interviews revealed that Wilma's parents had been good providers but had an authoritarian style. Wilma felt that as a teenager she had not had a voice in the rules set for her. Her father was a successful tax attorney and encouraged her to study accounting. Wilma was not interested in business but had not found a career path she enjoyed. When she finally decided to pursue an interest in music, she was frightened of leaving the security of her present job even though she had saved enough for a two-year graduate program at the local music college. She was so overwhelmed with the difficulty of the decision that she had missed two enrollment opportunities. With the deadline of the next term fast approaching, she sought help.

Wilma showed many characteristics of procrastination due to overarousal. First, she was generally anxious. She seemed to have a nervous system that was always going. It was extremely hard for her to relax, calm down after an upset, and sometimes to sleep at night. She worried a lot about herself and questioned her ability. What's more she felt that everyone else did too. She knew she was not coping well and felt that decisions were just too hard to make.

Wilma's treatment required four months of weekly sessions. The focus was to identify and tolerate strong emotions and to learn to calm herself with relaxation. She also learned to raise her self-esteem and to decrease anxiety by thinking about her decisions in a rational way. Finally she learned to systematize her work and to plan her time accurately.

Anxiety

Anxiety is multidimensional. It is associated with physical symptoms, such as racing heart, sweaty palms, and rapid breathing. It also may have a cognitive dimension in that it is linked with fearful thoughts about the future. Anxiety, in short, is unpleasant. Tasks associated with high levels of anxiety are avoided and the anxiety is terminated, at least temporarily.

It is not surprising that researchers have found substantial correlations between anxiety and procrastination. In 1984 Laura Solomon and Esther Rothblum reported that anxiety as a personality trait is related to procrastination. In a 1986 study, Rothblum, Solomon, and J. Murakami found that anxiety is significantly related to procrastination, and students who scored high on procrastination reported more physical complaints related to anxiety. High levels of procrastination also have been related to anxiety regarding social situations and taking tests.

One group of researchers, McGown, Rupert, and Petzel, reported an interesting and unique finding about procrastination and anxiety. They found that people who scored high on an anxiety scale either had the least or the most problem with procrastination. It seems then that for some, anxiety may be a cue to hurry up and get things done so that anxiety can stop. For others, anxiety is avoided by not doing the task at all.

Procrastination is an effective means of avoiding anxiety—up to a point. McGown and Johnson report that anxiety builds as a deadline nears, until the deadline can no longer be avoided. At that point, last-minute action occurs and the task is completed in a panic. In a related finding, Rothblum, Solomon, and Murakami report that students increase their studying close to the deadline and anxiety decreases. It is possible that once anxiety is faced—not avoided—that the task is no longer so threatening. Facing anxiety will be discussed in later chapters as a key technique for overcoming its harmful effect.

Fear of Failure

Clinicians working and writing in the field of procrastination have suggested that people who procrastinate do so because of a fear of failure. Studies show that 6 to 14 percent of people who score high on a measure of procrastination also report fear of failure. In particular, one study reported that students avoided tasks they felt they could not complete successfully. Fear of failure is reported to be related to depression, low self-confidence, and irrational beliefs about how successful a person should be.

Self-Esteem

Self-esteem consists of the statements you make to yourself regarding your ability, value, and effort. People with low self-esteem seem to be constantly critical of their performance. Most studies of self-esteem and procrastination show a relationship between the two to roughly the same degree. It seems that the harsher people view themselves, the less likely they are to take risks, face anxiety, or to be challenged.

It has been suggested that negative self-statements may be a form of making excuses. Judging your ability by impossible standards gives you an out. After all, if you're really not very good at something, why try?

Low-Conscientiousness and Procrastination

Unlike the overaroused procrastinator, who is constantly bombarded by stimulation and needs relief from it, the underaroused person is constantly seeking sensation. Boredom, restlessness, and high distractibility make it difficult to concentrate, to follow through, and to plan.

Hank is a twenty-year-old sophomore at a small southern college. His academic advisor referred him for counseling. Hank is highly intelligent. He succeeded in high school without really trying. Now that he is in college, he finds the courses more demanding. He never developed good study habits. He doesn't know how to plan a course of study for himself and he usually tries to study while watching TV. He is easily frustrated when he doesn't get the material on the first try and is beginning to wonder if he really is very smart. With the first sign of frustration, Hank is ready to pack it in and seek out some friends. Hank knows he is impulsive. He remembers the time he was faced with a history term paper and he and some friends went skiing for the weekend instead of studying.

Hank reveals in therapy that he had a problematic relationship with his father, a minister for a small southern church who expected a lot from Hank. Hank secretly rebelled throughout high school by cutting classes and drinking occasionally. Hank resents authority. He has transferred his feelings about his father to his professors, whom he feels are less intelligent than he. He gets secret pleasure out of defying them by putting off their requirements until the last minute.

Hank is a sensation-seeker. He isn't skydiving or bungee jumping, but he is looking for constant stimulation. He needs immediate feedback from his work or he becomes distracted by more pleasurable activities. Hank's course of therapy required six months of work. It was complicated by the need for him to identify his resentment of authority and to learn more adaptive coping strategies. Besides learning good study habits, Hank learned to tolerate frustration when feedback was not immediate and to increase his awareness of upcoming deadlines.

Conscientiousness

In 1995 Clarry Lay and Henri Schouwenburg found a strong relationship between conscientiousness and procrastination. Typically equated with responsibility or dutifulness, conscientiousness is made up of a number of factors, including the ability to manage time, self-discipline, orderliness, competence, self-control, and achievement motivation. The person who procrastinates because of low conscientiousness is aware of the things that "ought" to be done but cannot maintain concentration long enough to do them. Like Hank, he or she has low tolerance for frustration and difficulty delaying gratification. An impulsive shifting to more pleasurable tasks describes the poor work habits of this type of procrastination.

Rebellion

Rebelliousness is associated with procrastination and has been linked to styles of parenting, particularly the authoritarian approach. In 1991 Joseph Ferrari noted that adolescent girls who described both parents as authoritarian had a great deal of difficulty making decisions. Ferrari speculated that the girls used procrastination as a way to defy parents who used force to control behavior and who insisted on obedience. Jane Widseth writes too of the role of rebellion in students who put things off. She worked with a number of college students who procrastinated and rebelled against professors' authority. The students sometimes felt superior to the professor as well as frustrated by the need to submit to externally imposed demands. Clarry Lay also found that rebellious procrastinators felt that the demands placed on them were very stressful and that tasks were extremely difficult.

Perfectionism

Perfectionism commonly is assumed to be related to procrastination. It is thought that when personal standards are extraordinarily high, procrastination protects against experiences of failure. There is partial truth in this line of thinking. However, there are at least three types of perfectionism: self-oriented perfectionism, other-directed perfectionism, and socially prescribed perfectionism.

Self-oriented perfectionism involves self-imposed standards for performance and is not linked to procrastination. In fact, there is a negative relationship between setting your own standards and procrastinating on tasks. People who set their own standards are the most efficient and *least* likely to procrastinate. *Other-directed perfectionism* involves setting high performance standards for others and it is not linked to procrastination for the standard setter. *Socially prescribed perfectionism*, however, has a strong relationship to procrastination. This type of perfectionism concerns the ability to meet the standards set by significant others. It is related to the need for approval by others and the fear of failure. Those who score high on measures of socially prescribed perfectionism are sensitive to evaluative feedback by others. Procrastination serves the purpose of avoiding social disapproval.

Very often the fear of failure is derived from irrational beliefs about the standards that are set by others. Perfectionists don't fear the standards so much as the expectations surrounding the standards. This fear is a product of helplessness about standard setting. They feel that they have no personal control over the standard, and they have a sense of hopelessness about chances for success. Rather than attempt a rational problem-solving approach to the situation, the perfectionist shuts down and procrastination results.

Depression

Virtually all researchers on the topic of procrastination have found that depression is related to procrastination. They also note that depression and anxiety are correlated. Even when the influence of anxiety is statistically removed from depression scores, the relationship between depression and procrastination exists.

The relationship of depression and procrastination has been linked to socially prescribed perfectionism. The sense that you have no personal control over performance standards often results in depression.

Gordon Flett writes that an irrational belief that you *must* receive approval is the link to depression and procrastination. Those who score high on procrastination and depression are especially negative about their ability to get work done, their intelligence, and their physical appearance.

Calming the Storm

Procrastination has been linked to anxiety, low self-esteem, socially prescribed perfectionism, low conscientiousness, rebelliousness, and depression. Note, however, that these factors are only reported to be associated with procrastination; no one has found that they *cause* procrastination. For example, though feeling depressed *may* result in procrastination, it is equally possible that you may feel depressed because you procrastinate. The same may be true of self-esteem and anxiety. Furthermore, claiming depression or anxiety may be acceptable excuses for procrastination, while the real reason is that you chose some more pleasurable activity instead. Rebelliousness too may be a socially justifiable excuse for procrastination. You may find it more defensible to say you didn't do your job due to feelings of anger or resentment rather than a desire to watch TV.

Whether or not these factors cause procrastination or are just associated with it, the fact remains that intense anxiety, depression, or high distractibility are not pleasant experiences and cannot contribute positively to task completion. Calming the storm of emotion is an important factor in freeing up energy and attention to get things done. The chapters ahead will focus on smoothing the way through the thoughts, feelings, and behavior that interfere with task completion.

3

Stages of Change

People who have procrastinated habitually over a long period of time often wonder if they can change this behavior. They fear that procrastination reflects negatively on their character. They fear that they are inherently flawed or lazy. Fortunately, there is, at present, no reason to believe that procrastination is innate. Problems that often accompany procrastination, such as forgetfulness, anxiety, or low energy, *may* be inherited, but the behavior of procrastination is not. Procrastination is learned, and the habit of procrastination can be changed. The longer the habit has been practiced and the more pervasive the problem, the more difficult change can be. But you can learn to anticipate when problems will occur, interrupt maladaptive habits when they occur, and learn new adaptive behavior.

People do change, and in predictable ways. In their excellent book, *Changing for Good*, James Prochaska, John Norcross, and Carlo DiClemente outline the six stages of change. The authors studied thousands of individuals as they changed long-standing, difficult problems such as alcohol abuse, smoking, and gambling. They found that people used different techniques to accomplish their change but all proceeded through six recognizable stages in the process. Furthermore, the authors found that most people were able to overcome their problems on their own.

The first of the six stages of change is *precontemplation*. Change in this stage seems to be too difficult and is avoided. In the second stage, *contemplation*, you develop the desire to change but have little understanding of how to do it. In the *preparation* stage, you develop a plan to accomplish change, and in the *action* stage, you implement the plan. The fifth stage, *maintenance*, involves consolidating success, and the sixth stage, *termination*, occurs when your new habits are established and efforts to change can be ended.

Anyone endeavoring to change will progress through all six stages before the process is complete. The stages are stable, and you will experience them in order each time you attempt to change. It is possible to get stalled in one stage and the process will be derailed. It's also possible to slip back a stage or two when the change process becomes too difficult. Each stage is described here in more detail, and examples are given. Recognizing your stage of change and selecting appropriate techniques for that stage will determine the success of your effort to overcome procrastination.

Precontemplation Stage

People in the precontemplation stage of change, raise a wall of resistance against taking action. They deny the very fact that there is a problem. They rationalize problems—usually attributing them to someone else's hang-up. Patti, for example, likes to shop. Lately, the bills have been piling up with insufficient funds to pay. Patti first rationalized that it was the holiday season, and she had to keep spending in order to meet her family's expectations for gifts. After the holiday, the sales were good and she kept buying. Her husband tried to get her to ease up on the spending, but she dismissed his concern by thinking that he was cheap and stingy. When doubts began to pop up in her own mind, she always escaped them by getting busy with other things. Patti's behavior eventually put the family into financial crisis. She was forced to give up the credit cards and get credit counseling.

Patti put up a good fight against recognizing and dealing with her problem. She denied its existence, deflected criticism, and defended against her own bad feelings. Eventually though, she was moved by outside forces to change.

Precontemplators defend themselves well against recognizing a problem and the need to change. It is only by some outside force that denial is broken and change can begin. The forces that result in change are often the results of the bad habit—such as running out of money. Anniversaries, birthdays, and other major events also help people to break through denial. The start of a new year has long been associated with resolutions for change. Getting married or divorced also inspires people to get out of a rut. You have likely passed the precontemplation stage of change because you are actively reading this book on overcoming the problems of procrastination—unless you are reading just to pacify someone else.

A good understanding of the precontemplation stage still will be useful. Chances are you are in this stage for some problem behavior. As you work to overcome procrastination, you may find yourself slipping back into denial and defensiveness.

Once forced out of the precontemplation stage, gaining knowledge about your problem is vital. Studying the next chapter on procrastination traps—excuses—will be useful to keep you from slipping back into procrastination. At the precontemplation stage, it's also important to build your motivation for change. Chapter 6, on task-directed thinking, will give you a solid basis for positive goal-directed behavior.

Contemplation Stage

Jim has moved from precontemplation to the contemplation stage of change with his problem of anger. For years he denied any problem, stating that he was merely frustrated with all the blockheads he had to deal with. A heated argument with a traffic cop made him realize he was heading for trouble. Jim then began the contemplation stage of change. He began to seek knowledge of his problem. He read books on anger. He studied others around him for their level of anger and reactions to frustration. He reconstructed his past, looking for the origin of his behavior in his childhood and his parents' behavior.

Gaining insight into a problem is important for a self-change effort, but guard against prolonged contemplation. Being stuck in the contemplation stage is where most procrastination occurs. In a study of people's efforts to stop smoking, Prochaska and colleagues found that on average a person spent two years contemplating quitting before taking action. People in the contemplation stage eagerly seek knowledge and are willing to read and talk about the problem. Incessant reading and talking can lead to what is called *analysis paralysis*: efforts to change are postponed until the analysis is perfect or at least complete.

Change can be difficult. It is easy to see that remaining in the contemplative stage for prolonged periods of time offers a safe alternative to the fear of change. Movement from the contemplation stage occurs when your focus shifts from the problem or the past to the solution or the future.

To make this move, you must learn to manage the anxiety that accompanies change. The chapters on managing stress will be a focus for you as you move from contemplation to preparation or when you slip back to contemplation at any point in the change process. Motivation for making change also is important. Again, Chapter 6, on task-directed thinking, will help you remember why you want to change and help to decrease negative thinking. Finally, using imagery, described in Chapter 8 on stress management, is a key to motivating change.

Preparation Stage

In the preparation stage, activity toward change begins and expectations are raised. Mandy has been procrastinating on returning to school to complete her M.A. She lived with the denial of the importance of an advanced degree in the teaching profession while she raised her young children. She did, however, contemplate the benefits the additional salary and promotion opportunities an advanced degree would give her. Finally, when her oldest son began high school, she realized that she and her husband would be financially strapped trying to pay for their children's college. Mandy was thus moved to begin working on her degree.

The preparation stage is a time of decision making and commitment. Mandy must select a school and then prepare a plan of action to complete the work. Decisions need to be made about her daily schedule of work and home responsibilities. She must plan her course work and prepare to be a student again. Mandy's final decision is to make her degree a priority. Making a commitment to act is the final step in the preparation stage.

This book focuses on the stage of preparation. You will be asked to consider many change techniques and to choose the best ones for your problem of procrastination. This decision-making process involves active participation on your part. In the end you will have a complete plan to implement in the action stage of change.

Action Stage

The action stage is characterized by a great deal of activity toward the goal of change. Andrew, a dedicated workaholic, has discussed his stressful lifestyle and his failing health for years. He finally came to terms with his health problems when he turned forty. He then made plans to take a long-needed vacation. In the action stage, Andrew is in the process of getting his passport, picking up the tickets, packing bags, and so on. Such novel behavior will usually get the attention of those around you and bring comments about the change. This reaction can be unsettling, especially when you are experimenting with a new behavior yourself. Even well-intentioned comments can increase the anxiety level about change.

Because the anxiety involved in change peaks in the action stage, you will find the exercises offered in Chapter 8 on managing stress useful at this point. It is also important to combat interfering thoughts and not to get discouraged under the stress of changing behavior. Chapter 6 shows you how to replace irrational thoughts with task-directed thinking. Finally, the most work in the action stage will come from implementing the techniques that you decide to use from Chapter 7, on approaching the task.

Maintenance Stage

Once Tim finally decided to give up smoking, he had to work long and hard to quit. He procrastinated—contemplated—for years and finally quit when his boss died of a heart attack. Tim was well-prepared for the change. He chose a substitute habit—writing—and enlisted a few friends in a support group. Then he acted: he threw out all the remaining packs, lighters, and ashtrays, and posted No Smoking signs at his desk. And he succeeded. He hadn't had a cigarette in eighteen months. Tim started to feel pretty confident. He would now sit with his friends in the smoking section of a restaurant. Then when he found out his best friend had cancer, he started smoking again.

Tim prepared well for change and succeeded, but the common reasons for relapse bested him. Relapse, according to Prochaska and colleagues, is most often provoked by social pressure (sitting with friends in the smoking section), internal conditions (feeling overly confident), and special situations (the serious illness of a friend).

No new techniques need to be applied in the maintenance stage in order to preserve success, only vigilance for the conditions most often resulting in relapse. A little humility won't hurt, regarding the difficulty of change. Continued practice at clear, rational thinking and relaxation will help you maintain your new behavior.

Termination Stage

The final stage of change is termination. You are terminating the process of actively managing a bad habit. You can do this because you are no longer tempted to avoid or procrastinate. You have successfully spurred yourself on to face fear, and take action. Melissa, for example, procrastinated on organizing the books for her home-based floral business. She finally took action when she almost lost the business due to back taxes. Melissa then prepared and implemented a daily routine for herself that included accurate, thorough bookkeeping. She developed a system for managing her finances too. After years of successfully implementing this plan for change, it became habitual. She automatically finished the books and organized the store for the next day. She felt free of the fears of losing her business. She could relax and rely on her new work habits.

Termination is the goal of change efforts. It is possible to reach termination but most people do not get there the first—or even second—time. It has been estimated that 20 percent of people succeed on their first attempt to change. Recycling through the stages of change is the more common experience. When relapse occurs, you will not necessarily begin again at the precontemplation stage.

You may return to the contemplation stage to assess your motivation, or you may return to the preparation stage to formulate a new plan. Termination is possible, and with determination, knowledge, and a plan, it can be achieved.

Support from Others

Common to all stages of change is the importance of helpful, supportive relationships. Finding friends, family, coworkers, or a therapist to assist you in your change efforts is invaluable. It is important to select your supporters as warm, rational, concerned others. Honesty too is crucial for a supportive relationship. You need someone who will tell you the truth but in a kind, gentle way. Techniques for finding help are discussed in Chapter 12 on support.

The research on the stages of change is new and exciting information for those who are attempting to change. Knowing where you are in the change process can be comforting in what you may find to be a bewildering experience. Also, knowing the pitfalls of each stage can help you to prepare for these experiences. By knowing how change works and preparing for it, you are increasing your chances for success.

4

No More Excuses

For most people procrastination is a long-standing problem. The tendency to avoid the unpleasant has grown and developed and become habitual. Yet those same people were instilled with the values of hard work, accomplishment, and perseverance as children. Somehow, they must reconcile their current need for comfort with the mandates of childhood. Out of this dissonance, they have developed a host of reasons—excuses—for delay. Children, being unpracticed at this task, may resort to transparent excuses, such as, "the dog ate it." Adults, however, provide quite plausible reasons for their postponement, some so sophisticated they fool even the originator.

Making excuses for behavior is closely linked to procrastination. Excuse-making, called *self-handicapping*, has been investigated by a number of researchers. All have found a very strong relationship between making excuses and putting things off. There seems to be no difference between men and women in their tendency to make excuses. Joseph Ferrari interviewed shoppers at a mall during the holiday season. Late shoppers frequently cited the pressures of work as their excuse for procrastination. Self-handicapping also may involve how we set ourselves up to work—or not work—on a task. Clarry Lay found that college students who scored high on procrastination chose to have a distracting noise present when completing a performance task. The debilitating noise could then serve as an excuse for poor performance. Students who attempt to study while watching TV, adults who try to cook dinner while balancing the family books, or applicants who do not rehearse before an interview are engaging in self-handicapping behavior.

Excuses for procrastination tend to include external conditions (such as bad weather, broken equipment, distractions) or internal states that are transient and not really reflective of a person's overall ability, such as being tired or sick. Excuses serve as self-protection. You learned in Chapter 2 that procrastination is linked to low self-esteem and a sensitivity to criticism from others. People who procrastinate can protect themselves by establishing some kind of alibi for their performance. Self-handicapping is a way of avoiding responsibility for not performing a task we chose to do.

This chapter outlines some common excuses for procrastination. As you read, consider each excuse and how it applies to you and the task you have chosen to work on. Within, or at the end of each section, there are a number of self-assessment questions. Read and answer each question in the space provided. It is important to write your answers. Writing will encourage you to more carefully consider your responses.

I'm Not in the Mood—Setting Up Artificial Barriers

Dina is a 42-year-old bookkeeper. She has been working at a sedentary job and smoking up to a pack of cigarettes a day for twenty years. Dina has told her doctor that she wants to quit smoking. She's tired of the expense and it's becoming increasingly inconvenient to smoke now that her office has a no smoking policy and she must go out of the building to have a cigarette. Besides, smoking seems to be less and less socially acceptable. Many of her friends have quit. Dina has thought about quitting for a while. She decided not to attempt it during the holidays last year because of all the stress. After the new year was not a good time either because she had gained weight, and she was sure that if she quit smoking, she would eat even more. Dina finally decided to lose some weight and then stop smoking.

Dina set up several barriers to quitting. She planned to do it later—after the holidays—and then after some other event occurred first—losing weight. These are artificial barriers. They serve as excuses, a rationale for not responding to the present need, and as a means for avoiding the unpleasantness of overcoming a long-standing bad habit. Quitting smoking can be a very difficult task requiring many strategies for managing the urge to smoke and changing old behavior patterns. But first, it's critical to identify these obstacles placed in the path.

Artificial barriers need not only be events. Sometimes feelings may be set up as necessary for work to proceed. I frequently hear students in my classes on overcoming procrastination talk of not being "ready" to work. They feel they need to be ready, for example, to go out and look for new companions or a new job. Creative efforts are another area where people often impose the artificial barrier of "needing inspiration." Have you ever not written a letter because you were not in the mood? Writing holiday cards, completing applications, and calling friends are frequently postponed by people who think it is necessary to first feel like doing so. One young man came to see me because his marriage was starting to fail. He reported that his wife complained about the lack of romance in their marriage. He said he could see what she was talking about but he just didn't feel romantic anymore with all the stress of work, home, and child rearing. I strongly encouraged him to arrange dates or time alone with his wife even if he didn't feel like it. He reported later that sometimes the mood did follow once he got into an intimate setting with his wife. Other times the romantic mood did not strike, but they still had a good time together. The marriage, he reported later, improved much to his satisfaction.

Inspiration, readiness, and the like, are not necessary feelings for moving ahead and getting a job done. They are artificial impediments to completion. Most artists do not work from inspiration alone. Rather, they say their work is a craft—something to work on every day. Ernest Hemingway had quite the reputation for romance, but his literary success was not built on inspiration. He said what the public did not see was the four hours every morning that he spent working at writing.

Self-Assessment Questions

1. How am I setting up an "if" or "when" situation regarding my task?

   _____

   _____

   _____

2. What event or feeling do I consider necessary for work to begin?

   _____

   _____

   _____

3. Why is it really necessary for this event or feeling to occur first?

   _____

   _____

   _____

4. How could I proceed if this event or feeling never occurred?

   _____

   _____

   _____

I'm Too Busy—Getting Bogged Down in Trivia

A common stereotype of the procrastinator is someone lying in a backyard hammock while the lawn mower sits idle in the long grass. Laziness, or at least an attitude of unconcern, is often associated with not getting things done. People who procrastinate, how-

Self-Assessment Questions

1. On what activities do I spend more than three hours per week?

   _____

   _____

   _____

2. How does each of these activities relate to my goal?

   _____

   _____

   _____

3. How are these activities keeping me from my task?

   _____

   _____

   _____

4. Am I avoiding what is important?

   _____

   _____

   _____

ever, are not sitting idly by. Many who postpone important work are among the busiest people I know. They are just busy at nonpriority tasks. Robert Boice studied college professors who live by the motto "publish or perish." With such dire results of nonperformance, you would think that writing, producing, and publishing, would be a consuming task for these young professionals. Boice found that college professors in their first year of teaching actually spent about thirty minutes a week writing. He found, though, that two hours per week were spent in completing routine office or administrative tasks such as returning phone calls, looking up references, and so on. When interviewed, these professors reported that they were just too *busy* to get down to the work of writing.

Getting bogged down in what one of my students calls "administrivia" can be catastrophic for accomplishing a goal. The distraction from your task can take a more defensible form too. You may be deeply involved in charity work or other people's problems but still avoid your goals, be they personal or professional. The attention to nonpriority tasks can sometimes take on problematic proportions. Some people become so single-mindedly devoted to their distraction that it becomes an addiction of its own. William Knaus, author of *Do It Now*, refers to this as "addictivity"—an obsessive focus on one task to the detriment of other important tasks. Consider Mark, a 28-year-old software engineer, who always wanted to write music. Mark also has some ideas for songs and plays the guitar well. He wonders, though, if writing isn't just a little out of his league. He has no time to find out, since he spends all his time in clubs, work, or with friends.

The patterns of the college professors, Mark, and others like them who are very busy seem different from a lazy, unproductive person. These people seem to get a lot done but the problem is the same. They hide from personal discomfort associated with tackling their more important task by exaggerating participation in activities that are more immediate and emotionally more attainable.

I Can't Live Up to Your Expectations—Perfectionism

In this achievement-oriented culture, pushing the limits of human performance and striving for perfection are highly valued activities. A runner crosses the finish line and shakes her head dejectedly when she knows she has not broken a record. Or the skater sits breathlessly waiting for the judges' scores and looks disappointed when he receives anything less than a 10.

Chapter 2 reviewed three types of perfectionism and closely linked socially prescribed perfectionism to procrastination. When you strive to please others, rather than yourself, risk of failure and

---

Self-Assessment Questions

1. What am I expecting as a final result of my task?

_____

_____

_____

2. How can I accept my best effort even if not perfect?

_____

_____

_____

3. How can I look at the results of this task as a learning process not a judgment?

_____

_____

_____

_____

4. How can I let myself learn from the results of my effort?

_____

_____

_____

---

rejection occur. So much anxiety and fear can be generated that behavior is inhibited altogether.

Perfectionism first motivates and then excuses procrastination. Perfectionism begins with a desire to please others but results in a reason not to try. By doing a job perfectly, you hope to avoid rejection by others and personal feelings of incompetence. Unfortunately, the fear of being judged is inhibiting. If the task is a personal goal, it may never be attempted. If the task is set by others and a deadline is involved, procrastination occurs. The intense anxiety involved in facing the task can be overwhelming and can be avoided by delay. As the deadline nears, dread increases, and at some point activity begins. Because so much time has been wasted hiding from a fear of failure, little time is left for a good effort. The job is pulled off at the last minute and does not represent a best effort. You are left then with some sense of failure—which you started out to avoid. You also have some sense of relief. It's over. You scraped by again. Because you have in one sense succeeded, you are very likely to repeat this destructive, unfulfilling pattern again.

Overcoming a perfectionistic style is hard work—just like breaking any bad habit. It is a style of behavior developed to protect you, and letting go is not easy. You begin by recognizing your M.O. You will then need to develop a healthy habit or way of managing fear. The process requires a lot of specific habit-breaking tactics and constant, gentle encouragement.

It's Not My Fault—Blaming Others

Knowing who to blame relieves you of a lot of responsibility. Blaming others takes the focus off you and your actions—or inactions. For example, Catherine, twenty-three years old and currently unemployed, complains that if only her mother had been more encouraging, she could have taken high school more seriously and been better prepared to develop a skill and to find a job. Similarly, Rick, twenty-four and working as a paralegal, bemoans the obscurity of the college he attended and feels that if only he had gone to an Ivy League university he would have been accepted into law school. There may be some truth in each of these complaints. But it is also true that the reference in each event is in the past and cannot be undone. The problem lies in focusing exclusively on one small truth to the exclusion of all other influencing factors. It's easier to give up when it's not your fault.

The solution to this procrastination trap is a two-step process. First, it is necessary to recognize that you are shifting responsibility for your behavior to someone, or something else. Second, you must then look to realistic sources for bolstering your emotional supports and means for compensating for personal deficits.

Self-Assessment Questions

1. Who or what event do I find myself referring to when I
   think I cannot accomplish my goal?

   _____

   _____

   _____

2. How is it true that this person or event is keeping me *at*
   this time from pursuing my goal?

   _____

   _____

   _____

3. Do other people accomplish this goal even though they
   experienced the same negative influence as I?

   _____

   _____

   _____

I Have Too Many
Interruptions—Distractions

One form of self-handicapping involves succumbing to distractions.
When a job is difficult and a colleague interrupts for advice, it's a
relief to leave the job at hand. Or when you begin research for a
term paper, you find that an important book you need is out of the
library so you feel you really can't begin the project. Karen always
had trouble maintaining attention. She is a very energetic person
and wants to be on the move constantly. For her, housecleaning is
an endless ordeal. She would begin to straighten out one closet but
find herself going off on tangents as she dealt with each shirt, newspaper, or box she found. Instead of just sorting the laundry, she
would start to mend items. Then the telephone would ring and the

sorting and mending would cease. At work, Karen has the same experience. The office is chaotic and she relies on subordinates to rescue her when she can't seem to finish a project she has started. Karen excuses her behavior by saying she is overworked and rudely interrupted by others.

Self-Assessment Questions

1. What distractions have stopped work on my task in the past?

   _____

   _____

   _____

2. How do I turn away interruptions from my task?

   _____

   _____

   _____

3. How can I better respond to interruptions and be less distracted from my task?

   _____

   _____

   _____

I Can't Cope—Emotionalism

Becoming absorbed in the emotional experience of the task is another style of procrastination. Focusing on the emotions—usually negative—involved in facing and completing a job can be riveting. If you are avoiding something, it is likely to have strong emotional implications for you. Just the thought of calling someone to arrange a meeting, for example, brings back memories of other phone calls, some of them unsuccessful. Anxiety builds, and you turn your attention to internal voices warning of danger. As a result, the phone call is not made.

Robin is a middle-aged woman with a secure family and job. She has had a lifelong problem of getting along with her father. Robin's father is a product of the depression era and is frugal with his money and his emotions. Robin struggled for closeness with her

---

Self-Assessment Questions

1. What are the feelings I have about my task?

_____

_____

_____

2. How strong are the feelings?

_____

_____

_____

3. How am I letting the feelings interfere with getting the job done?

_____

_____

_____

4. Do I spend as much or more time thinking about the feelings than getting the job done?

_____

_____

_____

father but felt shut out. Now that Robin's father is in increasingly poor health, she wants to approach him regarding his wishes for the family estate. She wants to know where to locate papers, who to contact, and what her father's wishes would be. Robin thought about broaching this topic with her father for years. Each time though she became sad, then frustrated, then angry. She remembered so many previous attempts to talk when her father just changed the subject or left the room. The emotional pain involved in the task was so unpleasant that Robin terminated it immediately and consequently never resolved this conflict.

Separating how you feel about a task from the task itself can be a difficult job. It may take practice and a lot of honesty. It's also helpful to get feedback from someone you know and trust. You may ask a spouse or friend to help you to recognize the strength of your emotions or the extent to which they interfere with your task. It is important to know that how you feel about a job and getting it done are separate issues. You can work toward your goal while you are learning to deal with the feelings about it.

What's Your Style

You may recognize your behavior in one or several of the styles described in this chapter. The way in which you put things off also may vary from task to task. You may blame others when it is a personal goal, but set up artificial barriers in your work habits. You may have strong emotions that keep you from following through on some tasks, while you simply allow yourself to be easily distracted from others.

Regardless of your style or styles, you have learned to delay work in one or all of these ways. Your behavior has been determined by your learning history. Fortunately, because behavior is learned, it can be unlearned. The next chapter describes some of the negative thinking processes that stand in the way of action and introduces an exercise for combating them. The remaining chapters are devoted to teaching a variety of techniques—cognitive, behavioral, and emotional—that will enable you to stop heedless delay in accomplishing your personal goal.

5

Irrational Thinking
and Inaction

How you think about your task can influence what you do. Some types of thinking cloud your view and interfere with getting things done. For example, two students in the same class receive an assignment to write a paper consisting of a full 50 percent of their final mark. The first student reads the project description and says, "Oh man, what a job. I think this is due on the same day as my history exam. I'm going to have to clear out the next two weeks to get this done. Let's see, if I work on the paper first, I'll have more time near the exam to remember all those facts. . . " The second student says, "Oh man, I can't believe this. I can't get this done and study for all those other finals too. This is so stupid. Professors do this just to justify their own positions. I can't stand it. I'm going to fail because there is no way I can get this done."

The first student has an initial emotional reaction but doesn't dwell on the feelings about the task. Rather, thinking and planning begin. The second student eventually may get down to business and address the work in the assignment, but what a lot of negative emotion to wade through first! This student generates intense emotion, perceiving the assignment in a frightening, dreadful way, which is more likely to prevent his or her performance of the task.

As you already know, worry and depression are common problems among people who procrastinate. Fear of dire consequences and feelings of self-loathing often accompany putting things off. These feelings are so burdensome that they often lead to depression. Depression then produces more self-deprecation and inaction, and the downward spiral begins. The basis of the disturbing thought usually is not valid. Worrying typically stems from thoughts based on distorted reality.

Aaron Beck developed a theory of depression based on distortions often made in everyday thinking. He called these distortions "automatic thoughts" because they are experienced so readily and accepted so wholly that their truth is not often challenged. Automatic thoughts seem to be spontaneous. They are, in fact, quite ingrained. They may pop up anywhere and in many forms. Automatic thoughts may be full sentences, one word, or just a memory that flashes through your mind in response to a current situation. In addition to being telegraphic, automatic thoughts are highly personal. They are the product of your own experience. They are the conclusions and accompanying emotions you have drawn from your experiences. Depression is strongly linked to procrastination by many research studies. Recent information also confirms that the distorted thinking described by Beck is highly related to procrastination. People who procrastinate make many negative statements to themselves about their performance and their chances for success. They are particularly known to identify an unrealistic need for approval by others.

Being so spontaneous, telegraphic, and idiosyncratic, automatic thoughts are hard to stop. Fortunately, they are learned responses to the past and they can be relearned or replaced with new thoughts about the present and future.

Types of Distorted Thinking

Overgeneralization

The first example of distorted thinking involves extending the results of one (or a small number) of experiences to all similar experiences. For example, having one bad interview leads you to conclude that you *never* interview well and that you *always* will fail at interviews. The words *always, never, all, no one, every, none, everybody,* and *everyone* should be red flags to you as you learn to identify this type of dysfunctional thinking. The behavioral result of overgeneralization can be procrastination. You will be inclined to avoid certain situations since you think you can predict a negative outcome.

Labeling

Human beings have a strong tendency to name things. When the names are negative, they can cause emotional reactions and ineffective behaviors. Most people who find themselves putting things off conclude that they are "lazy" or, less stridently, have a "lazy streak." Even the gentle-sounding "procrastinator" is a negative, self-stopping label in a culture that values hard work and perseverance. The problem with labeling is that it can generate a self-fulfilling prophecy. When you assume a label, you are more than likely to behave in a way that is consistent with the label. It can be a way of giving yourself an excuse for your behavior. In addition to labeling yourself, you may label other people's behavior or a situation. Calling an assignment "stupid" or your boss "a power freak" can justify reactions of anger and resistance to action.

Catastrophizing

Catastrophizing means enlarging the outcome of an act or event to proportions beyond reason. It is the tendency to believe that the worst possible outcome will occur. For example, Sharon, a middle manager at a small hospital, worries that if her quarterly quality assurance report is not perfect, her credibility will be questioned and she will lose her job. Another example is Henry, an account executive, who believes that if he does not close the sale he is working on, he will lose face with his partner and eventually, the business. Notice that catastrophic thinking usually involves *if, then* statements. *If* _____ happens, *then* _____ will result. Fear of dire consequences can lead to behavioral paralysis. Sharon may never write the report, or she may wait until the last minute in order to avoid the feelings of fear involved in the project.

Henry, too, may procrastinate about contacting his customer as a means of avoiding rejection.

Lack of Control

Feeling controlled by forces outside yourself will leave you without reason to act. The essence of the control distortion is that you feel outcomes are beyond your influence. You are the victim. Consider, for example, the scientist who makes no effort to submit a much desired grant application because funding sources won't approve it anyway—since they only favor grants from the best schools; or the dancer who will not enter the competition because her style never wins. Subjective, unmovable forces control the events in your life—or so you feel. You have no need to try, and procrastination results.

Polarized Thinking

You are either a failure or a success, weak or strong, smart or stupid. In this style of distorted thinking, polar opposites are the only outcome considered for any experience. Shades of gray or varying degrees of competence are not considered. Polarized thinking can lead to perfectionism, since one mistake will ruin any effort. The student who receives an A- on a final exam feels like a failure because some answers must have been wrong. Or consider the cook who burns one roast and concludes that she is a failure in the kitchen. These conclusions would easily inhibit action.

Filtering

Putting your experiences through an emotional sieve results in filtering out any part of an experience that does not comply with your expectation. For example, your date compliments you on your appearance, sense of humor, and personal perseverance. She then questions your opinion on the national health care proposal and you return home sure that the two of you cannot get along. You believe that she thinks you are small-minded.

You have just filtered out a number of positive statements suggesting real interest in you as a person only to focus on a single statement questioning one political conviction. This very constricted type of thinking can lead to premature conclusions of failure and thus stop all goal-directed efforts. In contrast, broadening your thinking to take in all aspects of an experience can be encouraging and sustain behavior.

Mind Reading

You may feel that you have had so many bad experiences that you now can see them coming. These predictions usually take the form of knowing what people are thinking before they say anything. Patrick is sitting across from the bank manager who he has requested to see because his auto loan application was denied. Patrick notices that the manager looks at his watch frequently. Patrick becomes increasingly nervous and thinks the manager sees him as a deadbeat and not worth his time. Truth is, the manager is thinking about a lunch with his boss scheduled in fifteen minutes. Patrick, intimidated by the manager's aloofness, makes no real effort to plead his case.

Unraveling Distorted Thoughts

One characteristic of distorted thinking is that it is learned. No one is born with the thought, "It would be terrible if I wore the wrong dress to the party." It is not wired into the brain's circuitry. It is learned. The thought seems like a logical conclusion based on some similar experiences. Fortunately, because it is a learned way of thinking, it can be relearned. You have developed some bad habits of thinking, and habit control procedures are extremely useful in relieving you of this annoying, self-defeating thinking style.

Recognizing the Behavior

The first step in habit control is to become aware of when you engage in the behavior. You need to develop a sixth sense for when you are engaging in some kind of distorted thinking. A thought

Thought Diary

Date: _____ Day: _____

Time	Place	Activity	Others Present	Thought

Summary:

Frequently occurring time(s) _____

Common location(s) _____

Type(s) of activities _____

People present _____

diary is essential for this purpose. An outline of your diary might look like the one shown on the previous page. As with the Task Work Sheet, I recommend you make additional copies of this and keep a diary for a week or two.

By keeping track of the day, people you are with, and the activity you are engaging in, you can see patterns emerge. You may begin to notice that you consistently think self-defeating thoughts in the shower each morning before you even begin your day. Or you may detect that you consistently have negative thoughts when sitting through weekly staff meetings. Even if you determine that destructive thoughts occur at virtually any hour and with most people, you are making the first step toward change.

Replacing the Behavior

The second principle of habit control is to stop the habitual behavior as or before it occurs and to replace it with an adaptive behavior.

Beck presents a three-column technique for restructuring distorted thoughts. First, identify the distorted thought, then label it, and finally, replace the thought with a rational statement. Consider the following examples:

Thought	Type of Distortion	Replacement Thought
Don't believe anything she says.	Overgeneralization	Not everything she says is a lie. I need to check it out before I can believe her.
If this doesn't work out, I'm finished.	Catastrophizing	If this doesn't work, I'll think of something else.
In four cards he's sent, he's only signed one "love."	Filtering	He's sent me four cards, he must be thinking positive thoughts about me.

Thought	Type of Distortion	Replacement Thought
Only the boss's pets get promotions.	Control	I've done a good job. I deserve to try for the new position.
He's thinking I'm not very smart.	Mind reading	I don't know what he's thinking. I'd better ask.
This is just too hard for me.	Labeling	It's plenty hard—but not too hard.
I'm a social dud. I couldn't think of anything to say.	Polarized thinking	I said some things. I'll think up more conservative topics.

As part of improving your thinking habits, it is important for you to generate replacement thoughts for the automatic, negative thoughts you have. For practice, read the following distorted thoughts, label each, and write a replacement thought.

Thought	Type of Distortion	Replacement Thought
I hate them *all!*		
This assignment is stupid.		
I know she won't go out with me.		
Everybody here is so boring.		
I really messed up. I know I made at least two mistakes on the test.		
She makes the rules. I just follow them.		

If this gets
around, I'll lose
my job.

I was acing the
course, but since
that last test I've
lost it.

You are now ready to begin labeling and replacing your own distorted thoughts. The goal of this program is for you to begin to automatically have positive, self-starting thoughts about your ability. To accomplish this, you will need to change your behavior in stages. The first stage is to write out the irrational thought, label it, and then write a replacement thought. Practice this stage daily for at least a week. You will begin to get comfortable with labeling and replacing thoughts. You can then begin to do this three-step process in your head during or just after the habit occurs.

Practice, Practice, Practice

Practice at this second stage is critical. You must practice identifying, labeling, and replacing thoughts to the point where it is a very fluid, *easy* process. Stopping the irrational thought as quickly as possible is important. If you let negative, self-stopping thoughts continue for a while before challenging them, you will have essentially practiced defeatist thinking and made it more likely to occur again and again. By improving your skill and speed, you will find that the automatic negative thought is stopped almost before it occurs. Continue to formulate the self-enhancing statement, and let it be your guide to action.

Make copies of the blank three-column form on the next page for use on a daily basis. For each irrational thought you identify in your diary, label the distortion and then replace the thought with a rational statement.

Replacement Thoughts

Date:_____ Day: _____

Thought	Distortion	Replacement Thought

6

Task-Directed Thinking

The Beck method of countering irrational thinking you read about in Chapter 5 is designed to defuse self-defeating thoughts by replacing them with rational, goal-directed statements. Unchallenged, irrational thoughts have the effect of generating anxiety, worry, and depression. The behavioral result of restructuring your thought process is to clarify thinking so that you can use your thoughts to direct action, not avoidance.

Disarming Your Critic: Change Shoulds to Wants

Beck's technique was developed to treat depression and the frequently occurring behavioral inhibition accompanying it. Somewhat earlier than Beck, Albert Ellis, a psychotherapist, developed a similar system for challenging irrational beliefs. Ellis makes a meaningful distinction between two types of "should" statements and then relates this problem to procrastination. Some should statements are directed to the self and generate anxiety. For example, saying, "I should be able to express myself better" or "I should be able to handle the kidding from the guys at the gym" implies a concern about your adequacy and some self-deprecation for perceived incompetence. This may affect progress toward related goals. Feelings of incompetence are not a good basis for motivated action. Other forms of should statements—ought, must, need to—generate the same self-deprecating results.

Almost everyone defends making these self-punishing statements by believing that they spur you on to greater action. This is rarely true. Heaping shame on yourself results in feelings of failure, inadequacy, and incompetence—and is most likely to inhibit your desire to try. The Ellis prescription for overcoming this obstacle to action is to reduce the emotional imperative. Instead of feeling that you *must* succeed or that you *should* be happy, you reduce the demand to a want. Saying, "I want to succeed" and "I would like to be happy" reduces the emotional intensity and brings relief.

Should statements also may be externally directed. You may have firm beliefs about how the world *should* be. You feel that parents should care for their kids and that hard work should be rewarded. When these rules are broken, you feel anger. Anger may turn into indignation and a crusade for justice, or it may result in work stopping under protest. Consider Lucy. She is in charge of planning the party for her parents' fiftieth wedding anniversary. She feels that she *should* plan the party since she is the only daughter among four children. But she is resentful that she must do the work and she feels that her brothers ought to help. Her feelings of resentment based on a sense of injustice may result in procrastination. Some people are able to pursue their goals in spite of feelings of hostility. They typically stomp around grumbling that the work is too hard and that life is unfair. For others, hostility results in procrastination as a passive-aggressive way of fighting the perceived injustice. Lucy may slow down the work on the party, or "forget" to invite important people, or wait until the last minute to make arrangements. These actions are aimed to prove that she needed help and others should have known it.

Anger and resentment can result in passive-aggressive behavior and procrastination directed at the self, too. Studies link rebellion to procrastination. A closer look at a rebellious person reveals someone with ability who is rejecting achievement, usually out of a stubborn refusal to be driven by other people or forces. People who

Exercise

Consider the following examples of restructured should statements. Each replacement thought is more emotionally neutral and carries no threat of doom if wants are not met.

Thought	Replacement Thought
I should be able to handle this.	I want to handle it and I think I can.
I must get this promotion.	I want to get the promotion. I'll do my best.
I need to have his attention.	I want him to notice me.
She should be more considerate.	She is who she is. She is as considerate as she can be.
Police shouldn't give good citizens speeding tickets.	I want to be more careful of the speed limit.

Think of statements you are making about your task. Write the should statement and then rewrite it with a more balanced, rational replacement thought.

Thought	Replacement Thought
_____	_____
_____	_____
_____	_____
_____	_____
_____	_____
_____	_____
_____	_____
_____	_____

are rebellious and procrastinate also rate their tasks as very difficult, which increases the likelihood of making excuses to stop trying.

Parents, teachers, and friends may provide well-meaning advice, but their directives often take the form of should statements. When you're told you really need to get a job, or you really should try to take better care of yourself, or you really ought to get out of the house, etc., etc., etc., you first feel guilt and shame from the sense that you have been caught. You may next rebel and defend yourself by getting mad at the accuser. Procrastination results as you stubbornly refuse to look for work, get some exercise, or meet new people. This "biting off your nose to spite your face" syndrome is a tough one to get out of. One face-saving way to break this procrastination trap is to disarm your critic. You essentially take the sting out of the advice by making it your own; for example, you may say, "I've decided for myself to get out of these pajamas and go to class." In this way you have made the decision and it's clear that you are not being manipulated by others.

Frustration Tolerance: Facing Challenges

Unless you win the lottery, essentially all large, valuable rewards require work to obtain—work being effort over time. Behavior sometimes breaks down when the effort required is great or the time to reward is long. Low frustration tolerance is very much linked to the need for immediate gratification. It often results in an impulsive abandonment of intentions for some easier, less stressful task. Irrational self-statements creep in at these vulnerable times and can derail well-laid plans. The irrationality of these statements takes the form of exaggerating the difficulty of the task or underestimating your ability to deal with it. Problems in sustaining effort occur when you say, "This is just too much work" or "I can't stand it." You are giving yourself permission to quit. Usually you will turn to some less difficult or more pleasurable activity. Before you take this extreme step, try to evaluate the real difficulty of the task. Neutralize the emotion by reframing your statement away from the "awfulness" of the situation to a simpler descriptive thought. You can say to yourself, "This is hard. But is it too hard? I can't stand it? I am in fact standing it right now."

Exercise

In the following example, identify the irrational statements resulting from inability to tolerate frustration and rewrite them with a more neutral tone.

Nancy has resisted modern technology for a long time. In her new position as an account manager, she has finally accepted that she must master computer use. She's been through training and was advised to practice and to be patient, as it will take awhile to get the hang of it. Nancy didn't practice and now she faces a deadline tomorrow. Stomach churning, Nancy sits down at her keyboard. The system goes down but comes back up. She's saying, "I can't take this right now. I've got to get this done. How can this happen? I'm really going to lose it if this thing goes down again."

Thought	Replacement Thought
_____	_____
_____	_____
_____	_____
_____	_____
_____	_____
_____	_____
_____	_____
_____	_____
_____	_____
_____	_____

You may be thinking that there really are some situations in life that are too awful to stand. Contracting a fatal disease or a life-long debilitating injury are tough situations. Lots of people would see them as truly awful—not a distortion of reality. If this were the case, all people with physical or mental impairments would feel hopeless and depressed. People with these difficult problems may in fact look at them as just that—problems or challenges to be managed step-by-step and not to be magnified beyond emotional tolerance.

Combating Distractions: Emphasize Your Goal

People who are low in conscientiousness find it difficult to start or to finish a task because they are constantly distracted by events outside the task they've chosen. Many behavioral techniques are useful for refocusing attention, and they are described in other chapters. You can also use your thoughts to instruct yourself in focusing on the work to be done.

So far, you have been disputing irrational beliefs by first challenging the premise of the statement. You question the truth of your beliefs to see where and how they have been exaggerated. There are, however, situations in which your thinking is not based on a truth or untruth, but nevertheless it inaccurately directs your behavior.

Yvonne is preparing to study for her real estate license exam. She finds herself thinking one Sunday afternoon, "It's so beautiful today. First nice day we've had in ages. I don't want to study. I could be out with my friends enjoying myself for a change. I deserve a break. I've been working so hard." Yvonne is easily talking herself into exchanging her plans to study for an outing with friends. Too many days like this and Yvonne may regret not moving ahead in her career. She'll feel pretty low for trading a bright future for a few days of fun.

You can see that Yvonne's thinking is not distorted, but it is self-defeating. The premise is true—it is less than fun to study on a great day when she could be with friends. She could say, "So what. I decided to study and that's that." However, the temptation will reassert itself again and again. To increase your conscientiousness and strengthen your defense against distraction, you might prepare a list of reasons you want to do this task in the first place. Then commit the list to memory. Also, if you are in the contemplation

---

Exercise

List the negative statements you are making regarding your task. Be specific in the objections you raise.

_____

_____

_____

_____

_____

Next list the reasons you chose to do this task. What are the advantages of completing the job?

_____

_____

_____

_____

_____

---

stage of change, your list will help you to move on to the preparation stage.

Note that the advantages of completing the job do not have to be positive. I remember in one of my classes on overcoming procrastination, one young, working mother told me that she could never list reasons for wanting to make dinner. She did admit though that she makes dinner every night. But, she protested, she did it just so that it would be out of the way and she could do something more enjoyable! Wanting to get something done so that it is over is a perfectly good reason to do it.

Rebuttals for Yes, But. . .

You may now have begun to catch yourself in the act of making irrational or task-avoiding statements. You can label them, note the

---

Exercise

It's important to give equal time to the task-related statements. The more you practice thinking about your task, the more momentum and self-direction you will have. Practice the following techniques on a routine basis. Continue to practice until the task-directed statements become automatic thoughts themselves.

1. Write the reasons you want to complete your task on index cards. Post the cards in three places where you will encounter them often. Read the list slowly and thoroughly each time you see it.

2. Pick three objects you encounter every day, say, the billboard as you turn off to work each day. Every time you encounter this object, remind yourself why you want to complete your task.

3. List the advantage of doing your task on the Task Work Sheet.

---

emotion generated, and replace them with rational, goal-directed thoughts. Yet the job may not be done. You make positive statements about your task such as, "I do want to sort through the baby's winter clothes." You may remind yourself of the reasons you want to get through this rather boring task, and then you find yourself saying, "But I'm too tired. I'll do it tomorrow when I feel more like it." This one small word—*but*—seems to derail an otherwise rational process. David Burns, in *Feeling Good: The New Mood Therapy*, describes a process of "rebuttal." Essentially, a rational task-oriented comeback is needed for the excuse that follows each *yes, but* statement. You may also have more than one excuse—*but* statement—for your task.

Chapter 4 reviewed a number of common styles—excuses—for procrastination. You may have identified your own behavior in the tendency to blame others, wait for certain events to occur, find

---

Exercise

Consider the task you have chosen to work on. Think of your style(s) of procrastination and the type of but statements you make. Then formulate a rebuttal.

Excuse   **Rebuttal**

_____   _____

_____   _____

_____   _____

_____   _____

_____   _____

---

distractions, be emotional, or wait for inspiration. Your style often appears in the form of, "I could do it, but. . . " statements; such statements as, "I could work on my presentation, but (1) I'm not in the mood, (2) I can't find my text, (3) no one's prepared me for this, (4) I'm too upset, (5) tomorrow would be a better time."

Keeping on Track

This chapter and Chapter 5 outline a number of ways in which your thinking can irrationally influence your behavior. Various self-statements may generate anxiety, dread, or depression. None of these emotions necessarily results in procrastination, but all may. Just as your motivation for procrastination may be complex, your statements have several layers, alternately revealing deeper fears or shifting to avoidance of the tedious. For example, you may fear applying for grad school initially but then reorient your thinking and proceed to pick up the application. Once you begin to fill out the application, you may find yourself making excuse after excuse to escape the drudgery of filling out forms.

You have, however, now read and practiced techniques to reorient your thinking at every point of derailment. Canceling negative, anxiety-producing statements and reframing anger-oriented thoughts in self-starting, goal-directed statements beginning with, "I want to. . . " will neutralize emotion so that behavior can occur and tasks can be done. Other statements will increase your awareness of your goal and lead to increased conscientiousness and task completion.

7

Techniques for Approaching the Task

Regardless of your motivation for avoidance, you can apply certain techniques for approaching the task. Whether you postpone work out of fear of failure or because you are just not paying attention to what has to be done, you still will need to change your approach to the task. A new plan of approach also is needed regardless of your personal style for putting things off. Once you have caught yourself making one excuse or another, you will need to begin the behavioral work of facing the job, taking the first steps to get started, and sticking to it until the task is completed.

You may be familiar with the techniques described in this chapter. You may have tried some already, and you may have concluded that they do not work. You may be right. One particular approach technique may have failed in the past, but guard against overgeneralizing and concluding that none of these techniques will work. For example, you may have used the technique in isolation. One small approach behavior may not be all that is needed to overcome a large obstacle. You may need to put together several techniques—a package—that will help you get your job done. All of the techniques described in this chapter can be used together. Your package may include one technique or it may include all of them.

Experiment. Try some techniques that you have never encountered before. If you have been postponing work for a very long time, almost any behavior that is goal-directed will help you to overcome the inertia and get the job done.

All of the techniques in this chapter have one purpose—to make the job easier. Procrastination is avoidance of the difficult or unpleasant. Cognitive techniques discussed in Chapter 6 reduce the onerous nature of the job by reframing possible outcomes and focusing on positive reasons for the job. In addition to redirecting your thinking, you can reduce the amount of resistance to a job by clearly defining how much work it will take. Careful analysis of where, when, and how to approach a job greatly reduces the perceived difficulty of a task and leads to more task-related productivity. The techniques described in this chapter will form the basis of your action plan and take you through the preparation stage of change.

Before you begin this chapter, review your Task Work Sheet and, again, get a clear vision of the single task you want to accomplish. Review each technique described in this chapter and consider its application to your task. Think of ways you could apply the technique to the task you have chosen; then record your ideas on the work sheet.

Estimating Time

Very often, people who procrastinate are not good at estimating the time their task will take. Ironically, both underestimating and overestimating time are associated with procrastination. When you underestimate the time you think a task will take, procrastination is justified by thinking that there is plenty of time and no need to get started. When you overestimate the time, you may be intimidated by what you perceive as a large, difficult task and have trouble getting started.

Learning to accurately estimate how long your tasks will take is a useful skill. It will help you to plan for this task and others and may even relieve some anxiety and dread you have about getting started. Once you have an accurate estimate of the time needed to complete your task, you should set a deadline. Choosing a completion date gives you a sense of the reality of the task and also makes you accountable to yourself for your behavior. A problem sometimes occurs when you do not take your self-set deadlines seriously. Several of the techniques described here have built-in rewards and reminders that help to keep you on track.

Exercise

Consider the task you have chosen to work on throughout this book. Use one or more of the following methods to estimate the time you expect your task to take.

- Compare this task to a similar one you have completed. How much time did the previous task actually require to complete?

- Ask other people who have completed this task how much time was required.

- Keep a record of time you spend completing this task. Then start a log of time required to complete other tasks. Once you build up an inventory of tasks, you can use them as a guide to plan and schedule successfully.

On your work sheet, record your estimated time to complete. On your work sheet, record your deadline for completion.

Small Steps Technique

The small steps technique is the backbone of antiprocrastination work. As its name implies, small steps refers to breaking the task into smaller and smaller tasks. A very small task generates less displeasure and less avoidance behavior. One author refers to this technique as the salami approach. If you imagine eating an entire salami, it sounds pretty unappealing. But if you cut the salami into small pieces and eat them over a period of time, you could do it and gain some small satisfaction at every step. It's the same way with tasks you have been avoiding. The thought of filling out an entire mortgage application, completing a GED, or moving to another state can be overwhelming if taken in one piece. But if each task is broken down into small, discrete steps, you can focus on an emotionally and behaviorally manageable job.

Almost any task can be broken into smaller steps. The long lines at the post office every April 15 attest to the fact that filling out income tax forms is one task many people are likely to postpone. It is a daunting job, combining the tedium related to low frustration tolerance and the fear of making a harmful mistake. But to get going, you can break the task down into very small steps. First, pull out a folder of receipts. Next, organize the forms, and so on. If any one of these steps is too large and delay is experienced, that step too can be broken into smaller steps.

To most effectively use this technique, find the natural dividing points of the task and begin to tackle one small step. If you still resist, break the task down into even smaller steps until beginning work becomes easy. For example, Rupert finally decided to paint the kitchen, which was showing years of neglect. He thought about the task and planned to break it down into smaller tasks, such as cleaning, sanding, and painting. He then assembled his tools, took one look at the empty room, and became discouraged. Even the subtask of cleaning was too overwhelming for Rupert to face. He then listed the subtasks of cleaning the kitchen—walls, cabinets, ceiling, and so

---

Self-Assessment Question

1. What are the small steps that make up my task? List small steps below:

_____   _____

_____   _____

_____   _____

_____   _____

_____   _____

on. He felt confident that he could succeed at one of these smaller steps and work began.

Reminders

Your mother may have told you as a child that if you want to remember something, you should tie a string around your finger. This is not entirely bad advice. Providing some signal in your environment to prompt a future behavior is a standard behavioral technique. You have learned to associate all sorts of behavior with signals. For example, you stop at a red light and go at a green light. You avoid people who look really angry, and you don't tell off-color jokes in the presence of a grandmother. These are learned responses to what the world tells you will provide reward or punishment. It also is possible to create your own signals for behavior. If you procrastinate out of low conscientiousness, such reminders of your task will be a necessary component of your plan.

To Do Lists

To Do lists are a common way to organize a series of unrelated tasks. If you find, in looking back over your day, that you have not accomplished what you set out to do, you almost certainly need a To Do list. The list provides an organized way to increase awareness of tasks. It clarifies what really needs to be done. By selecting tasks for the list, you necessarily leave others off. You will be identifying and prioritizing your work, so spending a few minutes organizing the list can be very helpful. You may decide to list tasks in order of priority or in the natural order of getting them done. Once you've completed the task, it is very gratifying to take a pen and mark through it. Watching the list diminish can be rewarding.

Some students complain that they spend a great deal of time selecting tasks for the list. Some feel anxious about whether they are including everything; others report guilt over tasks not completed. This technique should not create any anxiety for you. It is a mental organizing step only. If you feel guilt or anxiety at this stage, reading Chapter 8, on relaxation will help.

If you decide to use To Do lists, you will need to determine the time frame for completing the tasks on the list. Lists are not meant to carry over week to week, month to month. Very often they are done daily, but you must decide the best time frame based on the tasks you select. By selecting tasks for the list and determining

Self-Assessment Questions

1. How would a To Do list benefit my work on this task?

_____

_____

2. How often should I write my To Do list?

_____

_____

Exercise

Complete the following To Do list for your task. List items in order of priority or in order to be completed.

To Do List

Date: _____

1. _____

2. _____

3. _____

4. _____

5. _____

6. _____

7. _____

8. _____

9. _____

10. _____

how long the list runs, you put a lot of mental effort toward your goal. You have begun the thinking—a major step in the task-oriented approach behavior that is essential to break the habit of postponement.

Schedules

Scheduling a time to complete a task from your To Do list has several benefits and is essential for procrastination resulting from low conscientiousness. You avoid the problem of saying, "I'll do it tomorrow," by identifying exactly when tomorrow is. It is more difficult to avoid the task as a specific time approaches. Scheduling postponed tasks is useful for busy people, as it is easy to get caught up in the events of the day and avoid your personal goal. People with lots of free time or the self-employed person can also benefit from scheduling. It is easy in these situations to fritter away blocks of time thinking you have plenty of opportunity later. The problem is that later never comes. Looking at your tasks in relation to other scheduled tasks will help you to determine how realistic it is to fit your task in at a selected time.

Self-Assessment Question

1. When will I work on my task?

_____

_____

_____

_____

Signals

Making the task conspicuous makes it more difficult to avoid. For example, leaving your briefcase by the door helps you remember to take it with you the next day. Or putting the laundry basket

Exercise

Complete the following schedule with all required activities for the week. Include time to commute, work, and so on. Be thorough. Fill in time on the schedule to work on your task.

	Sunday	Monday	Tuesday	Wednesday	Thursday	Friday	Saturday
7 am							
8 am							
9 am							
10 am							
11 am							
Noon							
1 pm							
2 pm							

	Sunday	Monday	Tuesday	Wednesday	Thursday	Friday	Saturday
3 pm							
4 pm							
5 pm							
6 pm							
7 pm							
8 pm							
9 pm							
10 pm							
11 pm							

in the middle of the living room floor reminds you to do the wash. If you catch yourself shoving the basket into the closet, you will need more than just this technique. One of my students wanted to learn a foreign language by using audiotapes on a long daily commute. He found that he just never reached over to the tape compartment to get them out. Using the signal technique, he began to leave them on the driver's seat. He then had to pick up the tapes to begin to drive. He had to take the first step in a chain of behavior leading to listening to the tapes.

If you are low on conscientiousness regarding your task, you need to establish several reminders to get the work done. Some reminders should specifically signal your task's due date. Mark all deadlines on your appointment calendar. Also post the due date at your office desk or where you study. You will find that you need to remind yourself of the deadline several times each day to avoid being distracted by more immediate pleasures.

Self-Assessment Question

1. What are the ways in which I can make my task more conspicuous?

_____   _____

_____   _____

_____   _____

_____   _____

_____   _____

_____   _____

Organizing Time Factor

You've learned ways of estimating the time a task will take; but looking at how you organize your job in time is also critical. As mentioned earlier, Boice found that many college professors postponed writing because they thought they needed a large block of time. Other problems in organizing time arise from the difficulty of estimating how long a job will really take. Underestimating time can lead to a real crunch at the deadline.

Swiss Cheese

Alan Lakein wrote a seminal book on time management, *How To Get Control of Your Time and Your Life*. He outlines a comprehensive system for identifying priorities and organizing work. One small but very effective technique he describes is called Swiss Cheese. This approach involves poking holes in a larger task by working on it at odd moments or in small bursts of time. The Swiss Cheese approach can be applied more widely than you may think. A writer, for example, can sit down for short periods of time and accomplish a lot. In the study by Boice, college professors were taught to write thirty minutes each day, and publication of manuscripts increased significantly. While you cannot clean your house in the spare five minutes before leaving for work, you can load the dishwasher. You will be amazed at how much you can accomplish in a few minutes.

Self-Assessment Question

1. What are the "odd" moments when I can work on my task?

_____   _____

_____   _____

_____   _____

_____   _____

_____   _____

_____   _____

Set Time

Somewhat the opposite of Swiss Cheese, the set time technique sets a fixed amount of time to work on a task. This can be especially effective when you are building a new skill. When you first learn a skill—say, playing the piano—you are not very good. Your immediate accomplishments alone are not likely to spur you on. Only after a lot of effort can you begin to play a recognizable song and be rewarded for your effort. To keep yourself practicing, you can set a fixed period of time for work. Do not quit before or go longer than your allotted time.

Set time can also be helpful when you are likely to begin a project and refuse to leave it to work on other pressing matters. Setting a fixed amount of time and then leaving the job can help ensure against neglect of priorities.

Self-Assessment Questions

1. What is the maximum amount of time I will work on the task?_____

2. What is the minimum amount of time I will work on the task?_____

Best Time

Decades of research show that human beings have a daily cycle of alertness and energy—called circadian rhythms. Most people are a bit sluggish around two o'clock in the afternoon. Energy levels pick up around four or five in the afternoon. In addition, each individual has a personal rhythm. You may find you are alert and energetic at six in the morning; others are not in full swing until midmorning. When you have spotted your best time to produce, use that time for your important tasks. The converse also is true. Use your least effective periods for more routine tasks.

Self-Assessment Questions

1. How alert and energetic do I feel at the following times:

    7:00 am_____

    10:00 am_____

       Noon_____

    2:00 pm_____

    5:00 pm_____

    7:00 pm_____

    10:00 pm_____

    Midnight_____

2. What is the best time for me to work on the task?

    _____

    _____

3. What is the least effective time for me to work on the task?

    _____

    _____

Organizing Place

In addition to time, your task has the dimension of place. Organizing your workplace can greatly influence the outcome of your goal. This is often a problem for people who are self-employed or don't have a highly structured work environment. Salespeople often tell me how easy it is to take a coffee break instead of moving on to the next customer. For people who work at home, it's easy to sit at the kitchen table in pajamas drinking a second cup of coffee well into midmorning. These problems can have serious consequences. One student in my class reported that he lost his travel business because he could not force himself to sit down and send out the bills—for services he had already provided! The goal of an organized workplace is to make your job easier. By carefully selecting and setting up your space, you can accomplish more, faster, and with less effort.

Designated Area

As discussed earlier, there are signals in the environment that tell you what behavior to engage in at the moment. Doctors use this to treat patients with insomnia. Patients are taught to associate bed with sleep. They are not to eat, read, or watch TV in bed. If they are in bed and not sleeping, they must get up. In this way, bed becomes associated with sleep and nothing else.

To develop consistent work habits, you want to develop a similar association between place and getting a job done. You should select a setting and then use this place only for specified work. Do not use the phone for personal calls, do not read the newspaper at the desk, and so on. Matthew McKay, author of several successful self-help books, checks into a cabin each time he needs to write. The cabin has no other distractions, and over time, his behavior of writing has become immediate and productive.

Self-Assessment Questions

1. Where will I work on the task?

_____

_____

2. Where will I not work on the task?

_____

_____

Tools

It's also important to have the tools that you will need before you begin the task. Be sure the pen has ink, the computer has disks, and so on. Providing yourself with good-quality or pleasing work-related materials also can make the job less aversive. If you're sitting at a chair that makes your back ache, you are likely to walk away from your task. Be sure to assemble what you need *before* beginning the job. If you are constantly getting up to find the white-out, the paper clips, and so on, you'll be frustrated much more quickly. If your avoided task is, for example, paying bills, put together a bill-paying box. Have stamps, checkbook, pen, and calculator all stored in one designated place so that once you start, you will have what you need. On the other hand, don't let the need for special tools be a reason for postponement. While special pens may make the job easier, it's not appropriate to postpone the task until you have them.

Self-Assessment Question

1. What tools do I need to have ready when I work on the task?

_____

_____

_____

Distractions

Waiting to be rescued is a common excuse for postponement. Rescue can come in many disguises, including distractions from the task. Have you ever used the phrase "saved by the bell"? Think about where you try to get your work done, and plan your work-place where you will be free of distractions—children interrupting, telephone ringing, a tempting refrigerator. One of the most common distractions is, of course, TV. Many students develop the bad habit of spreading their work on the floor or the bed and then attempting to study in front of the TV. The brain cannot concentrate on more than one topic at a time. Little real concentration and learning can occur if you are constantly interrupted or called on to attend to extraneous events.

By combining the dimensions of time and place, and selecting the right tools, you can develop good work habits. It is difficult to persuade yourself to remain with the plan and not succumb to the urge to revert to old ways. With practice, you will find it increasingly easier to use the new, more focused task-approach techniques. You will become more efficient and feel better about what you do.

Self-Assessment Question

1. What distractions do I need to eliminate from my work environment?

_____

_____

_____

Rewards

Overcoming procrastination is all about choosing long-term (bigger) rewards over short-term (smaller) rewards. This sort of self-denial makes managing this bad habit unappealing. The truth is, you do not have to forego all pleasure in the present for some promised future reward. Arrange your rewards to be incentives to work. You know, for example, that you would not show up for work very often if your employer mailed your paycheck in advance. You also know that teachers do not give recess on the promise that students will study later. While working toward a long-term reward, you can provide yourself with smaller, more immediate rewards to maintain progress. The point is to schedule the reward *after* the work is done. Rewards work very well in combination with the small steps technique. For example, Anne is making a quilt for a friend's baby shower. She works on it at night after work and she is tired, but she plans to do one row of squares each night and, after the work is done, to relax with a hot bath. The trick, of course, is not to let yourself slip and enjoy the reward before the work is done. If you find you have a problem managing temptation, choose a reward you do not have immediate access to. Give your best friend some money to hold for you and make an agreement to get it back after your work is done.

Rewards need not to be large or expensive. You may choose to purchase clothing, cars, or vacations as rewards, but smaller events can do. You may take a five-minute break just to daydream between piles of mail you must open.

If you are stuck for what to use as an incentive to work, think about what you do with your free time. In a 1965 study, David Premack noted that people could be rewarded by access to whatever they did frequently and voluntarily. Teachers, of course, have known this for decades and plan recess or fun activities to follow more difficult work. If you spend your free time watching TV, or reading the

Self-Assessment Questions

1. What could I use to reward myself for working on my task?

   _____

   _____

   _____

2. What problems will I have in managing my rewards? How will I solve these problems?

   _____

   _____

   _____

3. How often will I reward myself for working on my task?

   _____

   _____

   _____

newspaper, or talking to friends on the phone, each of these events could be used to increase task-related efforts.

Many people protest that they should not earn rewards for doing necessary work. They are full of self-blame and remorse for having procrastinated to begin with. Experts agree that it is helpful to make the process of change less painful. If you associate getting work done with receiving pleasure, you are strengthening your work habit—making it increasingly likely that you will complete your plan in the future.

Some psychologists recommend employing the opposite of rewards—punishment. That is, you may receive a reward if you complete a task on time and experience a negative event (punisher) if you do not. For example, you might decide to give money to a political cause you oppose or forego buying something you want. Punishment is not without its side effects. Frustration, anger, jealousy, and even aggression are among them. Because of this troublesome potential, I do not recommend it. Rather, learning to think positively, organizing time and space, and providing incentives result in a more productive work habit.

Self-Monitoring

Self-monitoring involves keeping a record of important behavior that you want to change. When procrastination occurs from low conscientiousness, keeping track of your behavior is a must. If you

Exercise

You have read about a number of techniques for approaching your task and making it easier to complete. Look back at the techniques and select three to five that you can apply to your chosen task. You may have identified more than five as pertinent, but it can be unwieldy to attempt them all at the beginning of your program. Careful selection and application of three to five is more realistic. Once you have narrowed your list, record them on your Task Work Sheet.

have been procrastinating on finding a new job, for example, keep a daily record of the number of minutes you spend job hunting. It can also be very useful to keep a log of time spent engaging in distractions. Most people are amazed at the amount of TV they watch when they take the time to keep a log. Putting your information on a graph can further increase the impact of your data as you see your behavior change. Sometimes self-monitoring is all that is needed to create change. Once you realize how little time you are engaging in task-related behavior, or how much time you are spending in avoidance, you may be moved to change. Most often, though, monitoring needs to be combined with rewards or other techniques described in this chapter to readily affect behavior.

8

Managing Stress

Research shows that a great many people who procrastinate suffer from stress. Those who procrastinate are vulnerable to stress as a result of their lowered self-esteem and perceived inability to cope and to control their lives. Gordon Flett and his colleagues studied procrastination and stress and found that people who score high on procrastination also report feeling hassled. In addition, they report that their hassles are persistent and have an impact on their lives. They feel unable to cope and are upset about their situation. Studies also show that these feelings of stress are related to the depression that is so often associated with procrastination, and both men and women seem to suffer equally from life's hassles. Finally, these feelings of constant stress are related to overall psychological adjustment and life satisfaction.

Understanding Anxiety

One form of stress related to procrastination is anticipatory anxiety. Stress may build as a deadline nears and the task is not started, generating fear that this time the job really might not get done. However, procrastination-related stress is more frequently related to fear of evaluation. It's not missing the deadline that's scary but how performance will be judged. Katrina is an aspiring actress. She has put on plays since she was small and went on to major in drama in college. She criticizes every performance she sees and feels that she could do better. But she rarely gets around to trying out for parts of any kind. She has a lot of trouble getting herself to rehearse thoroughly. When she does sign up for an audition, it's at the very last minute. The night before the audition, she usually experiences extreme anxiety and develops a migraine headache. She is then too sick to try out for the role and blames illness for her failure. Katrina has an intense fear of criticism. She has developed very high standards and doesn't give herself a lot of credit for her efforts.

People who procrastinate are usually self-conscious and worry a lot about how they are perceived. Social situations, including public speaking, are often particularly difficult. Those who procrastinate tend to determine their value as a person by how well they perform. Their fear leads to unrealistic, perfectionistic standards—the hope being that no one could possibly criticize them for not achieving impossible goals. The real result is that so much value is placed on outcome that all task-related behavior is shut down out of overwhelming fear.

Origin of Anxiety

Not all fear is maladaptive, and it does have an important biological origin. The human species would have vanished eons ago if a casual approach had been taken to food shortages or imminent danger, such as wildfires. Human beings developed what is called the fight-or-flight response. When faced with an immediate challenge, humans are biologically structured to fight or flee the opponent. When the fight-or-flight response is turned on, the body reacts in a powerful way by focusing all available energy on the goal of survival. Pupils dilate, making eyesight sharper; heart rate increases, giving more blood to the muscles for added strength; hearing becomes more acute; hands and feet feel cold as blood flow is directed toward large muscles. The adrenal gland also secretes corticoid, which inhibits digestion, reproduction, tissue repair, immune and inflammatory processes—all to give maximum energy to face the foe. When the fight-or-flight response is frequently turned on and for prolonged periods of time, the body is in a state of constant stress. Stress-related diseases may result. Katrina suffered migraine headaches, but arthritis, fatigue, and hypertension also may result. In addition, stress lowers the immune system response.

Many people feel that they need to be anxious in order to do well. They believe that without stress they will lose the drive to succeed. This sort of self-punishment does *not* facilitate performance. In 1950 Donald Lindsley studied the relationship of stress and performance and found that a moderate amount of anxiety did help performance on simple tasks but higher levels of anxiety resulted in diminished returns. Good mental and emotional conditioning is the best basis for improving performance.

Getting Started

The focus of this chapter is to reduce anticipatory anxiety and to enable you to live more comfortably in the present. By learning to calm your jangled nerves, you can access more of your real strength and apply it when and how you need it.

You experience stress in three areas: respiration, muscles, and thoughts. To calm yourself, you will need to gain control over all three. The techniques presented in this chapter give you several ways to master anxiety whenever it occurs. As with all the techniques in this book, you need to practice them until they become automatic. Because the techniques, when done correctly, can radically alter your body's response, it is important that you receive medical clearance before you begin. If you experience any effects that concern you, consult your physician before continuing to practice. Once learned, these techniques become the basis for strategies to prevent, reduce, and manage stress whenever it occurs.

Deep Breathing

Breathing is greatly affected by the fight-or-flight response. During stress, the body automatically begins to breathe faster. An increased rate of breathing is necessary to send large amounts of oxygen to the brain for mental alertness. In shallow breathing, your upper chest and shoulders move when air is inhaled and exhaled. In contrast, when your body is at rest, you breathe slowly and deeply. At the bottom of the rib cage, a sheet of muscles—the diaphragm—is located. You cannot see or feel the diaphragm externally. When breathing deeply, the inhaled air forces the diaphragm, and subsequently the stomach and abdomen, to expand. Deep breathing is sometimes called diaphragmatic breathing.

When you breathe deeply, more oxygen enters your lungs. The oxygenated blood leaves the lungs and travels to all parts of the body. Cells then absorb the oxygen and release waste products. If insufficient oxygen reaches your blood, cell purification cannot occur, and cells can be damaged or destroyed. You feel fatigued and out of sorts. Stress is harder to manage. Correct breathing, then, is essential for healthy bodily functioning as well as managing stress.

Progressive Muscle Relaxation

A second area of stress concentration is in the muscles. Two muscle systems exist in the human body: the smooth muscles, which control the heart and other vital organs, and the striped muscles, which are large muscles attached to the skeleton that control arm and leg

Exercise

To assess your breathing habits, lie down on a bed or padded floor. Loosen all tight clothing and notice how your body responds as you inhale and exhale. Time, in seconds, how long it takes you to inhale and exhale once. Notice, too, what body parts are moving as you breathe in and out. Continue in this position and monitor your breathing for five minutes.

Most people's breathing is shallow. Expect the time it takes you to breathe in and out to be about ten seconds if you have never practiced deep breathing techniques. The next exercise leads you step-by-step through the technique. Plan to practice the exercises on a daily basis. Mastery will require several weeks of practice.

Exercise

Find a quiet place where you will not be interrupted. Lie down and loosen all constrictive clothing.

1. Close your eyes, if you can, to increase concentration. If you cannot close your eyes comfortably, try to focus on some object in the room.

2. Breathe in through your nose and out through your mouth or nose.

3. Place your hands on your abdominal area. Breathe in slowly so that your hands are pushed out by your inhalation.

4. Notice your chest and shoulders. They should move minimally, if at all.

5. Breathe out slowly—even more slowly than breathing in. Be sure to empty your lungs completely each time you exhale. Your hands, still placed on your abdomen, will move down toward your spine as you exhale. Notice that your chest and shoulders do not move.

6. Continue slow, deep breathing for fifteen minutes. Continue to concentrate on your body's movement.

---

movement. There is no direct way of relaxing the smooth muscles, but relaxation of the striped muscle system will result in reduction of tension elsewhere and indirectly enable you to slow down a pounding heart.

Edmund Jacobson developed a technique for inhibiting anxiety and tension by training yourself to counteract them with a relaxation response. Jacobson's work, conducted in the 1930s, remains an integral part of behavior therapy today. The technique involves tensing and then relaxing muscle groups to achieve a state of relaxation. This process is repeated progressively through all muscle areas of the body and leaves you with a sense of "looseness" in the muscles and a feeling of calm.

Exercise

Lie down in a comfortable place with no distractions. Loosen tight clothing. Close your eyes if you can. If you need to open your eyes during the exercise, that's OK. Close them again and resume concentration on your muscle movement.

There is no necessary order of muscle groups through which you must progress. The list below begins with fists, but you can start anywhere. Do proceed in an orderly way because the relaxation in one group will carry over to adjoining muscles.

When you relax the muscles, be sure to let the tension go all at once. Do not slowly release the muscle. Hold the tension in each muscle group for five to ten seconds. Enjoy another five to ten seconds of relaxation in each muscle group before moving on to the next set of muscles.

1. Make a fist with both hands. Release tension.

2. Tense arm muscles by bending arms at elbows and squeezing muscles together tightly. Release tension.

3. Pull shoulders up toward ears as if to shrug. Release tension.

4. Push back of neck into pillow. Release tension.

5. Pull eyebrows up toward scalp. Feel tension in forehead and top of scalp. Release tension.

6. Squeeze eyes together tightly. Release tension.

7. Purse lips tightly. Release tension.

8. Clench jaw together tightly. Release tension.

9. Make swallowing motion and hold throat open.

10. Squeeze chest muscles tightly. Release tension.

11. Contract stomach and abdominal muscles. Release tension.

12. Squeeze buttocks together. Release tension.

Exercise (*continued*)

13. Squeeze inner thighs together. Release tension.

14. Pull toes toward knees. Release tension.

15. Point toes away from body. Release tension.

Following completion of one series, lie quietly for a few minutes and note your body's sensations. You will feel a little warmer. This is due to relaxation of muscles and consequent increased blood flow to extremities. You'll feel looser and maybe somewhat heavier. Repeat the series two more times to make three times per session.

Practice muscle relaxation daily for about six weeks. While you will begin to feel more relaxed almost immediately during the session, don't assume you have mastered the technique and discontinue practice. It requires extended practice before you can quickly and deeply relax your muscles for maximum benefit.

Once you have mastered progressive muscle relaxation, you can begin to use a simpler method to instruct your muscles to relax. A number of researchers have found that instruction to relax can be as effective as the progressive muscle exercises. Use the tensing and relaxing series until you become familiar with your bodily sensations and can recognize the feelings of relaxation. Following mastery, you may conduct your daily sessions by giving your body an instruction to relax each muscle group listed in the previous exercise. Continue to follow a systematic progression through muscle groups, and allow five to ten seconds of relaxation before moving on to the next muscle set.

If you practice both deep breathing and progressive muscle relaxation, you will find that they make a natural combination. Conduct your deep breathing exercise and then the muscle relaxation program. During your muscle relaxation, note your breathing patterns. If you revert to short, shallow breathing, return to your breathing exercise until you are again engaging in deep, diaphragmatic breathing. Then, return to muscle relaxation.

Visualization

Many people report that their relaxation efforts are thwarted by interfering thoughts. For some people who have suffered very traumatic experiences, the sensation of relaxation lowers the defenses and disturbing memories are relived. If you find that you become more anxious with relaxation, do not continue the exercises. Seek help from a therapist before resuming this work. If you are only disturbed by mundane types of interfering thoughts, such as what to have for dinner or whether the mail has arrived, you may significantly augment your relaxation efforts by focusing on a peaceful topic.

Creative visualization is known and used by many successful athletes. Many baseball, golf, and ice-skating stars use visualization

---

Exercise

1. Lie down in a comfortable place. Practice deep breathing and muscle relaxation until you feel calm. Use your imagination to see a soft shade of the color blue. Focus on the color. Let it occupy all of your mental energy.

   If you have difficulty imagining the color, place your palms over your eyes. Apply gentle pressure to the eyelid. You will see the color black. Focus on this color. You may see spots or lines of other color but focus primarily on black. Remove your palms from your eyes after a minute; continue to focus on the color black for five minutes.

2. Think of a time when you were very relaxed and happy. Maybe it was a day at the beach as a child. Or you may remember a relaxing Sunday drive through the countryside. Enliven this memory by seeing the colors present, feeling the sun on your back, smelling the air. Use as many senses as possible to remember the experience. Remember too the feeling of calm and quiet you had during the experience. Hold the image in your mind for five minutes.

Exercise *(continued)*

It's a good idea to have a number of scenes to draw on. You can then rotate them during practice sessions to avoid habituation and nonresponsiveness to the experience.

3. You also can use visualization to create future experiences. Once in a relaxed state, imagine yourself performing an avoided task with ease. See yourself in great detail. Picture what you're wearing, who else is present, and how the setting looks, feels, and smells. Continue the imagery from the beginning of your task until it is completed.

4. Completing your task may involve unforeseen difficulties. Again, visualize yourself going about your task. Use all of your senses to experience the setting. This time imagine that an obstacle has been put in your way. Imagine that you respond to the difficulty with calm, rational thinking. When you encounter the difficulty, engage in problem-solving and continue with your task. Continue this imagery until you have completed the job.

---

to train their performance and to assist concentration during competition.

Making a Tape

You have already seen how deep breathing can be followed by progressive muscle relaxation. Imagery easily can be added as the third step in the relaxation process. In this way all systems are focused on relaxation, and the total effect can be a satisfying, quieting experience.

You may find it helpful to make an audiotape of your relaxation exercise. Using a tape to guide you can be very helpful on days when your stress level is so high that you find it difficult to expend the energy to generate the instructions. Also, by using a tape you can become increasingly passive, letting the relaxation happen, rather than thinking of the next step. Making an audiotape using your own voice is a good idea—even if the sound of your voice seems strange at first. By instructing yourself successfully in relaxation, you are further empowering yourself to take control of your experiences.

Physical Exercise

A great way to reduce stress is to get some physical exercise. Just as humans evolved to need the fight-or-flight response, they also evolved to need a good deal of physical exertion. Sedentary lifestyles just aren't natural. If you're not getting regular exercise, you're adding to your problems of handling stress. Physical exercise causes the brain to release endorphins. They act as a natural painkiller and give you a feeling of calm. Low energy level is sometimes related to procrastination, especially in women. Increasing your exercise can also increase your stamina and available energy.

There are two kinds of exercise—aerobic and nonaerobic. Aerobic exercise is recommended for stress management because it produces the greater amount of endorphins and has long-term benefits of strengthening the cardiovascular system and increasing body metabolism. Aerobic exercise involves using the largest muscles of the body—buttocks and legs. Other muscle groups just don't have the *oomph* needed to get the heart rate going at a sufficient pace to have any real effect on other internal systems. Examples of aerobic exercise include running, jogging, and bicycling. Covert Bailey, a microbiologist from M.I.T., expounds on the benefits of aerobic exercise in his book *The New Fit or Fat*. According to Bailey, aerobic exercise must last twelve minutes (minimum) and be continuous. In addition, the pace must be sufficient to increase heart rate to 65 to 80 percent of capacity. Your doctor can help you to determine your optimal training heart rate.

Before each exercise session, it is important to warm up and then to stretch. Warming up usually consists of five minutes of very low intensity exercise. If your aerobic workout involves riding a bike, warming up would be five minutes of slow pedaling. Stretching comes next and involves stretching the muscles to be exercised. Each stretch should last about twenty to forty seconds.

It is important to check with your physician before beginning any exercise program. Once you do begin, keep a record of your workouts and try to increase activity gradually as your body can tolerate it.

Humor and Music

Another innate human response is laughter. When laughing, you will find it very difficult to worry. Laughter has a therapeutic effect on the body too. It causes muscles to contract and then to expand and increases circulation and respiration. Finally, the humor in your present situation can reduce the stress you experience. If you have difficulty seeing humor in the present, seek out funny movies, books, or friends for a good laugh.

Music that is chosen for its peaceful, calming effect reduces stress too. Music distracts you from your current frustrations and can stimulate positive emotions of joy, excitement, and solace. Music, like laughter, seems to be an innate human capacity and a natural form of therapy.

Bringing humor and music into your life, along with a routine of deep breathing, muscle relaxation, visualization, and physical exercise, can bring about long-term changes in body functioning and your ability to manage stress. Combining techniques or using them all will create the best result. Also, by becoming proficient in all techniques, you can use them as the situation permits and feel that you have a great store of skills to draw on.

Exercise

On your Task Work Sheet, list the stress management techniques you will use to cope with the anxiety and frustration of completing your task.

9

Procrastination and Studying

All-nighters and *cramming* are terms that will strike a chord with any student. You probably aren't surprised to learn that significant problems with procrastination have been found in extensive numbers of studies in academic settings. Some studies assess junior and senior high school students, but most focus on college students. Hill and colleagues investigated the frequency of procrastination on college campuses at large and small, private and public institutions in the East and Midwest and found that 27 percent of students surveyed—across all colleges—reported frequent procrastination on academic tasks. Other reports place the incidence of procrastination at 22 to 33 percent or as high as 41 percent! No differences have been found between men and women in their reports of procrastination. Procrastination does vary by task. Writing term papers poses the most difficulty—46 percent of students report procrastinating on this task. Students also report procrastination on reading assignments (30 percent), studying for exams (28 percent), attendance (23 percent), and on admission tasks (11 percent). Problems with procrastination seem to get worse—not better—with increasing years. Seniors report more difficulty managing study behavior than do freshmen. Faculty too report struggling with procrastination. One study indicated that 18 percent of faculty members report always or nearly always procrastinating. Note, however, when faculty behavior is observed, rather than self-reported, the incidence is much higher.

Students also report that procrastination causes practical problems for them in their academic careers. Most significantly, several studies document the relationship between procrastination and lower GPA. Students who procrastinate are not getting as much out of courses they take, and the lower GPA can affect post-grad plans for applying to science, engineering, law, medicine, and other graduate school programs, as well as negatively influencing prospective employers.

Causes of Procrastination Among Students

On surveys assessing the problems of procrastination, most students endorse several reasons for postponing their academic work. Anxiety is frequently cited. Students are particularly fearful of tests and other situations in which their performance will be evaluated. Performance anxiety stems from a fear of rejection and criticism. The academic setting, with its imbalance of power between teacher and student, may encourage this fear. Faculty set the criteria and typically sit in sole judgment of a student's work. Students often feel at the mercy of faculty standards and can be bewildered and anxious when assignments seem vague or grading systems are not explained. Students also lack assertiveness when dealing with their academic careers. Students report a real reluctance to seek out professors for additional help or even clarification of expectations. This only feeds the feelings of uncertainty and dependency on an external authority.

Given some students' fear of external evaluation and their lack of assertiveness, it is not surprising that a rebellious form of procrastination occurs. Students struggling with the uncompromising demands of faculty assignments may deliberately delay in order to feel some control over their actions. William Sommer suggests that the procrastination is carefully calculated and work is delayed until the last possible moment. Furious activity then occurs, and most often the student succeeds by pulling off the assignment at the last minute. A certain triumph is felt at beating the system. However, the cost is high: neglect of other pleasures and responsibilities, loss of sleep, and a performance that is less than capacity.

Low conscientiousness also is a basis for academic procrastination. Students who are low in conscientiousness typically have poor study habits and lack self-discipline and control. These students can be found partying or watching videos the night before exams. Students who lack conscientiousness seem to lose their notes, books, and assignments; have trouble settling down to study; and give up quickly when the material is difficult. Students of this type are often forgetful and lose track of time and the deadlines set for papers and tests.

Regardless of whether procrastination is based on anxiety, rebelliousness, or low conscientiousness, the problem remains that something other than academic work is consuming time. It helps to identify these alternative choices, which you may choose to substitute for studying. Dating and socializing provide immediate gratification and obscure the distant rewards of good grades and their associated opportunities. Older students may find that the compelling demands of family and work lead to avoidance of academic work. Awareness of these sidetracks and determination to refuse the easy way out is a good first step in redirecting your behavior to the task of studying.

Like all people who procrastinate, students have the best of intentions to study hard and to do well. Jeremy began the spring semester firmly resolved to study hard, keep up, and to bring his GPA up to 3.0. Things started off well enough; he even went to the library a few nights a week for a while. After the first month, his efforts slipped, but he felt he deserved to slack off a little—he had been working so hard. Then his girlfriend increased her demand for his time, he picked up a few extra hours in his job at the campus bookstore, and suddenly he was behind in English lit, biology, political science, and French. Then the flu hit. The semester ended up pretty much like all the others. Jeremy felt angry, discouraged, and uncertain about himself.

Jeremy began with good intentions, but what he really needed was a plan. Lack of planning as an organizational aid is a common fault among people who procrastinate. Planning has a few simple components that need to be thoughtfully combined: awareness of time, events, and resources. Then the interrelationship among these variables must be understood and organized. Planning also moves from the longer term to the shorter term. Good planning is like using binoculars effectively. You are constantly sliding your focus between distant and near objects.

Academic Planning

William Sommer identifies three overlapping time frames that determine academic life: the college career, semester, and day-to-day living. The semester has been the focus of most studies on overcoming procrastination. George Semb, professor of human development at the University of Kansas, has spent over twenty years working with students, teaching them to pace their study throughout the academic term. Semb reports great improvement in student performance when rewards or penalties are provided for keeping up (or not keeping up) with class assignments. Harold Ziest, Ted Rosenthal, and Glenn White also report improved academic performance among college students when positive reinforcement and good study habits are taught. Leon Green found similar results. Mary Harris and Amaryllis Trujillo found that students as young as junior high school could benefit from these procedures.

To make an effective plan for completing academic work, you need a clear sense of the amount of work to be completed and the amount of time available to complete that work. It's important to plan at the semester level and to translate each course requirement into a deadline. Then, arrange deadlines in a realistic way and monitor them frequently. Remember too that plans need to be revised based on experience. The key, of course, is commitment. Changing old habits is hard work, and only a full-hearted effort will succeed.

Planning Calendar

To begin, find a good-sized calendar covering the months of the semester. Each date should have enough space to write identified priorities for that day. Within the first week of classes, sit down with course outlines and write in the assignment due dates on the semester calendar. Next, write in dates for special events, holidays, vacations, and so on. Then, add routine commitments, for example, work schedules, choir practice, or dance class. You will already see that some weeks are going to be more difficult than others.

Setting Deadlines

The next step is to take each assignment and break it down into smaller tasks. For example, if a midterm is due on introductory psychology, generate a To Do list outlining each subtask leading to the exam:

To Do

1. Read chapter 1 pp 1–50.

2. Read chapter 2 pp 51–104.

3. Read chapter 3 pp 105–160.

4. Read chapter 4 pp 161–200.

5. Review chapters.

6. Quiz with study partner.

Next, you will need to calculate how much time each task will take. In their helpful book *Studying Smart*, Diane Scharf and Pam Hait provide a simple formula for calculating study time. They estimate it takes four minutes to read and underline a page of text. So the fifty pages of chapter 1 will take 200 minutes or about 3 1/2 hours. Based on the estimated amount of time required to read and underline a chapter, designate a due date for completing this task on your planning calendar. Continue this process for the remaining three chapters and write in due dates on the planning calendar. Reviewing text is estimated to take 2 minutes per page. From this, you can calculate how long it will take you to review your text. You will have to estimate some tasks, such as practicing quiz questions with a partner, based on your experience. Calculate a reasonable time and then set a deadline for this task too on the planning calendar.

Continue to generate To Do lists for each assignment due this semester, and then set a deadline for the smaller tasks. Write deadlines on the planning calendar. In doing so, be sure to note how each of these self-imposed deadlines relates to all other scheduled tasks.

Self-Monitoring

Make a few copies of your schedule. Post one where you regularly study and carry another with you throughout the day. At least once each day, you must review the schedule. Count the number of days until your next deadline. If you miss a deadline, reschedule it on your planning calendar. When rescheduling a missed deadline, be sure to note its impact on other deadlines. Keeping in constant contact with your plan is critical to making this an effective strategy.

Effective Studying

Effective studying depends on the development of a reliable set of study habits. The less time or tolerance you have for studying, the greater your need for efficiency. Try implementing one or a number of the following effective strategies for developing good study habits.

- *Choose one place—and only one place—to do your studying.* This study setting then becomes associated with effective work and will come to automatically trigger concentration.

- *Plan the amount of time you will spend studying.* In general, fifty-minute sessions are effective. If you find yourself drifting off, take a two-minute break from your study setting and then return to your work.

- *Monitor your study time.* Keep a daily log of the number of minutes spent in actual concentration.

- *Be prepared.* Be sure the lighting is adequate, seat comfortable, and materials available before you begin your session.

Rewards

All of the information on changing behavior confirms that change will not occur unless there is a payoff for doing so. The reward for changing study habits is fairly distant—better grades, increased employment opportunity, higher salary, for example. These delayed rewards are usually not enough to sustain the effort it takes to change old habits. You will need to provide yourself with some activity that is more immediately gratifying. If possible, follow a successful study session with some social activity, preferred TV program, or other activity you enjoy. It is equally important to stop and note to yourself that you did accomplish your goal. Registering your success will, over time, change your perception of yourself and your ability.

Support

Studying need not be a solitary activity. Finding a study partner can improve your compliance with a study schedule and make the task more pleasant. It is important, though, to choose a partner who has study skills as good as—if not better than—yours. Don't study with someone who is easily frustrated or quits early. Exchange planning calendars with your study partner and ask about upcoming deadlines and levels of preparedness.

Assertiveness

Assertiveness means pursuing your interests in a nonaggressive way. If you feel that your assignment is not clear or you need some additional help, don't be afraid to ask for it. Some students hesitate to approach professors about assignments. They postpone their own work, hoping that their questions will somehow come clear. Be active. Call your professor, seek an office appointment, or make an effort to speak up in class. A lot of self-coaching and anxiety management may be necessary to get this done, but it will be worth the effort. There are a number of good books that can help you improve your assertiveness, if you want to pursue this further. I would recommend *Your Perfect Right* by Robert Alberti and Michael Emmons or *When I Say No I Feel Guilty* by Manuel Smith.

Rational Thinking

Clearing your head of irrational thoughts can greatly increase your motivation to study. Such thoughts as, I must stand out in this class or I have to ace this test to pull up my GPA, imply catastrophic events if not fulfilled. Using your thoughts to direct the behavior at hand is far more effective. Try to guide your study behavior by asking yourself questions about the material. Make encouraging remarks to yourself as you work, such as, "Got that problem solved" or "One more paragraph to go—good going."

Another thinking pitfall that almost always leads to procrastination is feeling that you must be in the right frame of mind to study. You do not need to feel inspired or ready in order to get assignments done. You may also tell yourself that you are too tired, depressed, or anxious to study. You will often find that once you get going, the negative emotions disappear or at least do not prohibit work.

Anxiety is common among students. Each semester contains numerous occasions on which performance is judged. Competing demands of social, academic, and sometimes family life can create a lot of stress as well. Developing a two-step stress-management program that includes positive self-talk and some form of physical relaxation will be helpful in combating these feelings. The first component involves engaging in calming, goal-directed self-talk. You will find instructions for developing these statements in Chapters 5 and 6. Second, some form of physical relaxation is needed. Given the sedentary nature of studying, physical exercise is the best remedy, but if you have a physical limitation, progressive muscle relaxation can be highly effective too. Chapter 8 covers these topics in more detail.

Career-Level Procrastination

The focus of this chapter has been combating procrastination on a day-to-day basis. But academic delay can occur at the career level too. Some students postpone selecting a major or choosing a dissertation topic for unnecessarily long periods of time. Delay at this level involves fear of making a mistake. Any attempt to choose a direction is accompanied by a mental list of failures that could result from making a choice. Delay also reflects a personal sense of inadequacy. You feel that you are somehow not capable of making a good decision for yourself. You don't trust your judgment and you fear the judgment of others. Working with an academic advisor to clarify goals and options is a good first step. Cognitive interventions will be useful to overcome anxiety, anger, or other derailing thoughts. Develop a set of positive self-supportive and goal-directed statements to sustain you as you take the risk and choose a plan of action.

10

Procrastination
at Work

If you have ever waited for a company to replace your defective merchandise or issue a credit, you know that procrastination occurs in the business world. When service or money is involved, procrastination may result in short-term savings for the business. But usually the cost of procrastination is high. It results in diminished productivity requiring extra hours of labor and ultimately dissatisfied customers. With a fast-paced, bottom-line approach to the business, companies do try to assess and screen out persons with obvious problems of procrastination. The techniques for assessment are not, to date, very good, and people do get hired and then exhibit productivity problems. Many companies invest time and money in training to increase productivity. Training often focuses on time management, and results are usually insignificant or not maintained after the consultant is gone.

The cure for procrastination in the business world is good leadership. Management must model and reward good work habits and support staff efforts to improve performance. The process of change will require, as always, sustained effort over time.

Procrastination at the Organizational Level

As in other areas of life, procrastination at work occurs for a variety of reasons. It may be one person's problem or it may be endemic in the organization. Organizations have a culture with both written and unwritten rules. The company motto may promote service as the goal but actual on-the-job behavior may be different. An organization may, in fact, sanction procrastination simply by tolerating its existence. If people who procrastinate get promotions and raises, then the company does not value getting things done. Your organization will tell you how serious it is about procrastination by setting performance standards and then handing out perks and rewards for meeting them.

In small, tightly run businesses, employee performance is noticed. A bad job will be obvious, and usually the person responsible can be identified. However, in larger organizations, more employees and bigger bureaucracies contribute to greater chances of widespread procrastination. Even when detected, procrastination in a large organization can be difficult to resolve. Supervisors may be distant and overloaded and not able to focus on one employee's problem. When the supervisory process fails, companies must follow a number of steps of disciplinary action that must be extensively documented. By the time the process is complete, the employee may have transferred or quit the position. The employee and the organization have lost valuable time, productivity, and opportunity to learn.

Procrastination at the Personal Level

Wes has been head of facility operations at a large office complex in the Northeast for years. He has amassed an amazing amount of knowledge about the operations of every heating, cooling, and cleaning system in the place. When there is a crisis, Wes is in his glory. He can usually figure out and fix the problem before any real damage is done. The problem is that between crises Wes's performance is less than exemplary. He can't find tools, he loses maintenance request slips, and his crew is usually out on coffee break, since they have no clear assignment for the day. Wes knows he needs a filing system and a way of prioritizing repair slips. His boss doesn't want to fire someone who has been in the job so long, and especially someone with his ability to solve problems on the spot. He just wants Wes to get his act together. Talking hasn't helped and he is now seriously considering demoting Wes to a maintenance position. Wes has tried putting himself on a schedule, but each time a crisis occurs, he is thrown for a loop. Wes is discouraged, embarrassed, and increasingly harder to work for.

If you have ever supervised a Wes, worked for him, or sat in your office shivering while the air conditioning ran rampant, you know what problems procrastination at work can create. Many people who seriously procrastinate are out of a job. But most, like Wes, hang on, usually due to some performance characteristic that is greatly needed by the organization. It is interesting to note that employees who procrastinate can be very intolerant of the problem in others. When adult students who also were employed were presented with a scenario of a procrastinating employee, the most frequent solution to the problem was to fire him or her.

Procrastination at work often is the result of individual employees' personal problems. However, a number of features of the work environment or the task itself can cause needless delay. The most common of these is the lack of clear deadlines set for task completion. Your project manager may indicate that the report is due after the first of the year. Unless you have some vested interest in that project, the lack of a specific deadline is an invitation to procrastinate. Similarly, there may be no clear guidelines for your role in a project. You may, for example, receive a memo to be mindful of safety factors and to help avoid accidents. But without specifics of what to report, how, and when, you are not motivated to action.

At other times, there is so much pressure to make a deadline that other tasks are neglected. You feel that some things just have to wait, but the problem is that the tasks kept waiting usually then become crises and, in turn, absorb all of your time.

Another task-related dimension that can result in procrastination is the perceived difficulty of the job. You may find that you postpone very easy work such as filing memos. It seems just too trivial to take your time—until your desk is buried in them. Or you may postpone getting started on large, lengthy, or difficult tasks. When the job is hard, any available excuse can support your avoidance. So if the deadline is unclear, or you feel you must wait for

Self-Assessment Questions

1. Do I have piles of papers, reading materials, and so forth, on my desk? Do I say I will get around to reading them but never do?

   _____

   _____

   _____

2. Do I have only a vague idea about when a project should be done?

   _____

   _____

   _____

3. Can I work on one thing at a time? Do I get irritated when my focus is interrupted?

   _____

   _____

   _____

4. What new behavior can I practice at work that will address my particular problem with procrastination?

   _____

   _____

   _____

role clarification, you are ready to procrastinate. Altering your thinking about the difficulty of the task and breaking the job down into small steps will be essential to break out of the procrastination trap.

You can address procrastination at work due to project or personal disorganization by practicing new behaviors and sticking with them until they become habits. Here are some suggestions:

- Touch each piece of paper once. It is obvious that you cannot receive and respond to an entire proposal the moment it arrives. But there are a number of routine tasks that do not ever need to reach the "in" basket.

- Delegate. Whenever possible, delegate a task to someone with more time, interest, or expertise in an area.

- Know as much about a task as possible. Ask questions of people involved and talk to others who have done this work in the past.

- Set your own deadlines for each subtask of a larger project.

- Keep a current To Do list so that you can avoid letting things slip while you overfocus on one task.

Burnout

If you find you are constantly postponing easy and difficult tasks, and especially if you used to get these done, you may be experiencing burnout. Burnout is a result of an imbalance in the work and leisure aspects of your life. You are not getting enough variety and pleasure to rejuvenate you. First, look at how you work. Are you barreling through the day without a moment to relax? You may even be skipping a lunch break and just eating at your desk. You may have false expectations about your colleagues' commitments, and you may be trying to carry the load for them.

It's also important to look at your whole life situation. You may not be getting enough from your personal life. You may be expecting work to sustain you in an unrealistic way. If you are experiencing a decrease in your ability to effectively get things done, a number of steps can be taken to revitalize your interest before you conclude that it's time to quit.

Self-Assessment Questions

1. Am I finding a general disinterest in work that I previously enjoyed?

   _____

2. Is this disinterest specific to work or is it carried over to my personal life?

   _____

3. What is one change in my behavior that I can make at work to revitalize my interest?

   _____

   _____

   _____

4. What is one change in my behavior that I can make at home to feel more rested and ready for work?

   _____

   _____

   _____

- Examine other areas of your life. Be sure that you are getting enough rest and recreation. You may need to revise your leisure program.

- Begin your work day by setting firm but reasonable goals.

- Pace yourself. Take breaks; use them as rewards for completing a set amount of work.

- Focus on the present. Keep your mind on your work instead of dreaming about nonwork activities.

- Associate with colleagues who are enjoying their work and maintaining productivity.

Rebellion

The work environment, like school and parental relationships, has an imbalance of power between employer and employee. Depending on the skills and experience of each party, this relationship can be satisfying. However, very often the supervisor is somewhat anxious in the position and then behaves in a controlling, impersonal way. The subordinate feels hurt and threatened, and rebellion can occur. Direct confrontation is rarely advisable with employers, so the employee rebels by controlling behavior that he or she has a say in—procrastination results.

Early in my career as a psychologist, a client, Richard, came to see me about problems with anger. He worked for an automobile club, providing roadside services. He felt that he got all the really bad assignments. He was always sent on the farthest call and in the worst weather. Richard was furious with his dispatcher, and he rebelled by procrastinating in leaving for the call and losing the paperwork on return. The focus of the therapy was slanted toward controlling anger, but recognizing and coping with the tendency to procrastinate at work and home was helpful to Richard.

Recognizing and controlling your anger can be one of the most useful skills you will ever acquire. Inappropriately expressed anger can result in a variety of misfortunes, from family breakups, to loss of employment, to traffic tickets. Treatment of anger is beyond the scope of this book, but good books are available on the topic. I highly recommend *When Anger Hurts: Quieting the Storm Within*, by Matthew McKay, Peter Rogers, and Judith McKay. My students have reported over the years that it contains helpful, effective advice. The following points provide some preliminary guidance on anger control:

- Don't kid yourself about being angry. You may try to deny it and call it something else: blowing off steam, venting, expressing frustration.

- Before you act, think of the consequences. Do you want to pay the price?

- Think the situation through. What you want to do is prevent this situation from happening again. Try to figure out how you got into the situation and how it can be avoided in the future.

- If you feel you are going to say or do something that will hurt someone, then remove yourself from the situation and think.

Self-Assessment Questions

1. When my boss discusses a task with me, do I feel myself getting angry?

   _____

2. Does it feel good when I procrastinate, at least temporarily?

   _____

3. Do I often feel like expressing anger at work to my boss, colleagues, or subordinates?

   _____

4. Have I had to repair a relationship or project at work due to my expression of anger?

   _____

5. What can I do at work to:

   a. detect that I am feeling angry?

   _____

   _____

   _____

   b. handle anger more appropriately?

   _____

   _____

   _____

- Use words to communicate with others. Choose words that describe *your* feelings, not ones that accuse others.

Fear of Failure

Fear of failure can also create procrastination at work. You are probably familiar with informal chatting that goes on in every place of work. Chances are you have witnessed a colleague picking apart the behavior of a coworker—reviewing and downgrading everything from appearance to performance. It's possible that you identify with the colleague being skewered at the moment. You imagine yourself in his or her shoes and dread becoming the subject of similar attacks. These feelings are then carried over to a time when you must complete a task. You may obsess about doing the job perfectly or postpone it altogether, then complete it in a last-minute rush. Your motive is to avoid the pain of failure.

Kelly is a graphic artist at an advertising firm in Boston. She is talented and has produced some excellent, successful ad campaigns. She becomes so nervous at the thought of showing her work to the account manager that she always misses her deadline. She stays up all night, drawing, arranging, and rearranging her production over and over and over. Kelly finally gives up and hands something in but cannot feel good about it. When her proposals are sent back for revision, she is devastated, and the process of procrastination starts over again. This kind of fear can be managed and the procrastination trap avoided in a number of ways:

- Preempt the criticism. Test the waters with your ideas. Instead of waiting to unveil a completely finished product, talk to colleagues about your plans and ask for feedback.

- Based on feedback you are getting about your plans, try to think of the criticism you might hear, and practice a rational reply.

- Think of the worst response you can get. Then imagine yourself tolerating your adversaries with calm composure.

- Expect criticism. No matter how good your idea may be, your colleagues will need to challenge you in order to understand your work. Or they may feel a need to compete with you for their own survival.

Self-Assessment Questions

1. Do I feel a mixture of anxiety and dread even thinking about having my performance evaluated?

2. Do I avoid the boss or supervisor, for fear that my approach will not be welcome?

3. Do I avoid going for promotion or special assignments? Do I tell myself that I wouldn't get it anyway?

4. Do I criticize others' performance? Do I need this in order to protect myself when I am judged?

Employers Who Procrastinate

Needless to say, working for someone who procrastinates is a frustrating position. Your employer has great power over your livelihood, and it is in your interest to keep the relationship on good terms. This can be difficult when you've seen, time and time again, how projects are postponed until the last minute; then nail-biting frenzy begins. You may be caught up in this pressure-cooker atmosphere, and it's difficult not to be thinking how all of this could be avoided if only the boss could plan ahead. If your resentment lingers, you could find it spilling out at other times. You may find you're less tolerant of your boss in general. This behavior can be perceived as insubordination and weaken your position in the firm. You also may begin to procrastinate. Finally, your employer's procrastination can create problems for you if he or she is the type that blames others for delays and related problems as a way of avoiding responsibility and harm.

Taking Assertive Action

Confronting the boss can be delicate, and it is usually inadvisable. To avoid feeling helpless, follow these suggestions for assertive, rational action:

- Learn as much as possible about the project. Think ahead to where the project could get stalled and offer suggestions in advance of the crunch time when everyone is feeling testy.

- Do as much of your own work on the project as early as you can. When crunch time occurs and you are suddenly given even more work to help others catch up, you will at least have your own done.

- Know that the last-minute rush is going to occur. Prepare yourself for the inevitable. You may need to do a lot of cognitive restructuring to avoid getting overly angry.

- Offer to help when and where you can.

- If you feel you cannot approach your employer about the problem of procrastination, talk to someone closer to the boss and discuss the problems created and how to solve them.

Employees Who Procrastinate

When your employee procrastinates, it may be a result of a number of personal problems or there may be aspects of the work environment that exacerbate the problem. The employee may bring to the job a history of battling authority, low conscientiousness, or anxiety, all of which can result in procrastination. Any predisposition an employee may have toward procrastination can worsen in an organization that tolerates the behavior. Be aware of aspects of the job, such as vague expectations or fuzzy deadlines, that can become easy excuses for someone predisposed to procrastinate.

Combining Understanding with Clear Goals

As an employer you want to increase productivity and decrease procrastination. There may be times when you think it's easier to do it yourself than to struggle with someone who procrastinates, but never do the job for the employee. In doing so, you only rescue and reward him or her and perpetuate the problem. You want to help the employee to deal effectively with the problem.

First, try to understand the reasons behind the delays. Assess the employee's state of change. Is the employee unaware of the problem, actively trying to change, or slipping back into an old habit? Base your intervention techniques on the employee's readiness for action. Also consider whether the employee is engaging in procrastination due to anxiety or low conscientiousness. If the problem is anxiety, a more supportive, encouraging approach can help. If the problem is one of low conscientiousness, you will need to be clearer on expectations and consequences for continued procrastination. Follow clear guidelines with encouragement for effort. Ultimately, it is the employee's responsibility to change. You should not become overly involved in the change process. There are a number of specific steps you can take to work with the employee who habitually procrastinates:

- Meet with the employee to review the problem. Try to understand the reasons for procrastination. Discuss the repercussions of delay on you, other employees, the business, and the employee.

- Focus on the problem of procrastination rather than emotional or personal problems.

- Be specific about expectations and set clear deadlines for the task.

- You may want to develop a contract with the employee for completing a specific task. Be sure to list employee behavior, deadlines, and consequences.

- Use rewards when progress is made. Even words of encouragement can be very effective.

- Bring the problem of procrastination into the performance appraisal system. Again, set clear standards and explain the consequences of procrastination.

- If your organization has an employee assistance program for dealing with such problems, refer the employee to it.

One last point—be sure to let the employee know that you can separate the issue of procrastination from the person. The employee should know what skills and traits you value in his or her performance. Help the employee to avoid equating self-image with procrastination.

Challenges of Self-Employment

Pat recently left an established real estate firm to work on her own. Initially she was excited about the challenge of running her own business and glad to get away from office politics. She planned to convert a spare bedroom into an office but had not gotten around to it just yet. She was working at the kitchen table. The table could no longer be used for meals, so she ate most of them standing up at the kitchen counter. At first she really liked not having to dress up every day, but now she was lounging in slippers and robe until noon. She started off with the paper and a cup of coffee and was increasingly postponing the start of the work day. Pat was adrift and didn't know how to regain control.

Working at home appeals to many people at some point in time. Long commutes, difficult employers, fixed salaries, and an established routine can be wearing. But the freedoms that come with self-employment can quickly feel like chaos if you lack self-discipline.

Getting Organized

If you've made the move and started your own business, or simply made arrangements to work for your company at home, you know there are lots of distractions that can lead to procrastination. Working outside the home provides many cues each day to signal work behavior. Getting out of bed at a set time, dressing, shaving, driving to work, and signing in all condition the response for work to begin. At home, you don't have clear signals and behavior can slip. The following suggestions outline a number of steps that can provide the structure for a work day.

- *Determine a work schedule.* Many self-employed people are loathe to do this since escaping a nine-to-five routine is one reason they wanted to work for themselves. A work schedule does not need to be rigid. You can set the schedule for different hours on different days to accommodate priorities for that day. Be sure to include breaks—when and for how long. Developing your own policy for taking days off and sick time will avoid procrastination for days at a time.

- *Develop a ritual for beginning your work day.* This ritual may involve dressing in "work" clothes, turning on the computer, turning off the coffee pot, and so on. Your routine should involve two or three behaviors executed in a set order that signal to you that it is time to work.

- *Establish one place to do your work.* It's important that you set up a work space that is comfortable and only associated with the work you do. The setting will become a trigger for work behavior.

- *Set goals for the day.* Determine to complete a set number of hours worked, calls made, or money generated before quitting.

- *Use a To Do list every day.* Prioritize your tasks on the list and work on high priorities first.

- *Set up a ritual for the end of the day.* Again, include two or three behaviors that can be linked together to signal that work is over. Turning off the computer and lights, closing books, and cleaning your desk may be included. As with any work, once completed, it is important to turn to a different type of activity in order to be rejuvenated for the next day.

Breaking the procrastination habit at work can be a good training ground. At work you have less personal investment in comparatively defined tasks, and there is a real motivation to succeed—or at least to keep working. Once your antiprocrastination skills are improved in the work environment, you will be better prepared to take on more difficult personal risks.

11

Procrastination at Home

Mary is a twenty-nine-year-old middle school teacher who is very competent at her job. Mary's lesson plans are up-to-date. Students receive graded papers in a timely manner and her classroom is well organized. Mary is often chosen for extra committee work by her principal. She is a highly regarded teacher. At home, though, Mary seems to be a different person. The house is a mess. Mary seems to save everything. She has stacks of magazines going back seven years. The closets are stuffed with old, outdated clothes. Drawers are full too—crammed with items, many of which don't work. Mary sometimes thinks of cleaning the house, but the job seems overwhelming and she can't decide where to start. She agonizes over each item, deciding whether some day it might be needed. Laundry is a problem. She hasn't had to resort to buying new clothing because everything is dirty, but she's worn some things more than once. Mary doesn't have friends over because of the mess. Mary's social life consists mainly of the numerous charities in which she participates actively. Mary can't understand how she turned out this way, especially since her mother was so neat and organized. She frets about her predicament but feels that right now she is just too busy to do anything about it.

Mary's situation is common. Many people perform competently at work or school but are ineffective in their personal lives. The academic and work environments impose some structure on what's to be done. There is either a professor or boss directing projects and setting standards and deadlines. The work and school environment also have a rhythm. School semesters begin and end with the seasons, and vacations are timed to occur with holidays and summer. There also is a beginning and ending to the work day. Work or studying can be left behind for a time and you can escape—to your home.

At home great stretches of time must be structured. Coming home at the end of the day, you must decide whether you will shop and then make dinner or make dinner, shop, and then study. The course of events is up to you. Unlike work or school, there is no external authority (with a bottom line to back it up) telling you what the priorities and sequence of events will be. Unstructured time is like a pit of quicksand for those who procrastinate. When hours stretch ahead, it is easy to think that you have plenty of time to get started. With this type of thinking, you will usually underestimate the number of distractions that will occur or the real amount of time needed to complete the task. If you plan to pay the bills right after watching the news, you are not planning for the unexpected phone call from your mother or settling a fight between the children. The night is soon over and you're thinking that you'll do it tomorrow. Weekends pose even more difficulty. The stretch of time can seem endless. Some people feel overwhelmed and even depressed about the amount of time to fill on weekends. Others are pleasantly procrastinating and thinking, "Well, there is always Sunday."

Many people feel that they really have very little free time. There seems to be a constant demand for your attention—from children, community work, jobs, house, holidays, and so on. Studies show that Americans today have several more hours per week of free time than they did forty years ago. A major obstacle to using this free time in the home environment is the number of time-wasting temptations freely available. Today many homes are multimedia playgrounds. Television is the primary consumer of free time for Americans. A 1985 survey reported that Americans spend 38 percent of their free time watching TV, and that was before most homes had access to cable with up to 100 channels. Other media compete for free time too: CDs, videos, video games, and most recently, the PC. PCs are opening new vistas of entertainment, allowing users to play games, pursue topics of interest, and talk to others.

The problem with such consumption is that no useful product results from the time spent. People engaged in these activities for long periods of time do not report a sense of fulfillment. Rather, they feel that they have accomplished little and have a sense of loss of free time.

This chapter focuses on a number of aspects of personal life that are often left undone. Specific suggestions for getting started on these areas are included. Also included is a discussion of living with someone who procrastinates—your child or spouse. Guidelines for motivating others are reviewed as well as specific points about how not to make the problem worse.

Taxes

Judging by the long lines at the post office on April 15, procrastinating on completing income tax forms is a common experience. The post office stays open until midnight to accommodate the crowd. The local TV station usually takes a camera crew to the scene and interviews a number of taxpayers. When asked why they waited so long, the reply usually takes the form of being busy with responsibilities or reluctance to pay Uncle Sam before absolutely necessary. Some vow to do better next year, but others admit they'll probably procrastinate again.

You may be tired of the last-minute rush and the frantic feeling that you have left something out which may cost you later. Paying taxes is a prime task to be put off because it combines several ingredients for procrastination. The task of preparing returns is tedious for most people. It involves reading complicated, dry instructions and making careful calculations. It's also anxiety provoking because mistakes can cost you money now and later. If you want to take on the task of beating the April 15 deadline, consider the following ideas.

- Delegate. If you can afford it, pay a professional to compile your return. The results may be advantageous to you in terms of added deductions, and the fee for the service is deductible too!

- Form a self-help group of neighbors or friends. Set a series of dates and have everyone bring their forms, pencils, receipts, and so on, and work together, lending consolation as needed.

- If you go it alone, set a deadline well in advance of April 15. Write it in your appointment book. Break the task into small steps. You may begin by just stacking forms, receipt folders, and so on, in one place. Your next small step may be to place the address label at the top of the form. Each step can consist of filling in one line of the form. Also, if you are going to get a rebate, start planning how you could put it to use.

- If you are filing jointly with your spouse, sit down together before the first of the year and plan who will be responsible for each step and set mutually acceptable deadlines.

Holidays and Special Events

Holiday time, whether it's Christmas, Hanukkah, or the Fourth of July, adds demands to an already stressed system. Special events, such as weddings (especially your own), anniversaries, and birthdays, can be added to the list. These times produce a lot of ambivalent feelings for most people. On the one hand they bring a welcome relief from the pressures of everyday life and provide a source of memories of family and friends. They also generate a lot of work. If planning is left undone, the sense of frantic unpreparedness can completely overwhelm the positive aspects of the experience. A young woman who was planning her wedding joined one of my classes on overcoming procrastination. She was completely overwhelmed by all of the details and couldn't find a place to start. She used planning her wedding as her task to work on throughout the course. She started with a To Do list, bought calendars, appointment books, and with a lot of encouragement from her classmates, left feeling in control.

Holidays and special events are sentimental times. People often feel that they need to act out of inspiration. It seems unfitting to sit down and just write out holiday cards or thank you notes. Many people would rather wait until they are in the mood. The problem with waiting is that the inspiration may never come and meanwhile, time is flying. It's better to approach these tasks as you would any other job. Once preparation is underway, you'll have time to make an inspired phone call to a long-lost friend and just enjoy the feelings that come with the time.

Another source of conflict is the sense of obligation to make the occasion memorable. You can feel a heightened sense of responsibility and turn this pressure into a need for perfection. Add these pressures to the existing demands of life and the fact that you're supposed to look and feel happy, and it's not surprising that many shake with anxiety but do little to deal with it. Facing the inevitable and getting started early is the only hope.

- Give yourself permission to let some routine chores go undone for a time. To do this without feeling undue guilt, you'll need to think ahead to all the required tasks. Prepare a complete To Do list for all aspects—parties, gifts, cards, and so on—and prioritize what really is needed during this time.

- Once you have your priorities set, start scheduling due dates on a calendar or in your appointment book. Keep your eyes on the date for the upcoming event and adjust your schedule frequently as needed.

- For holidays and events that require gift exchanges, join a savings club for that purpose. When the season comes around and you don't have to worry about the expense, you'll be relieved of one large pressure.

- Start early. Again, when gifts are involved, pick up items throughout the year. Don't worry that you may find it cheaper elsewhere or that it's not exactly what you wanted. Fight perfectionism.

- Delegate. Have a family meeting and divide up the responsibilities.

Social Life

People who are otherwise organized at home may procrastinate in their social life. People who procrastinate are often depressed. A key signal of depression is withdrawal from others and from activities that promise fun or enjoyment. People who procrastinate also typically are anxious. Remember that procrastination often involves fear of evaluation and performance anxiety. Those who feel that they are constantly being evaluated are likely to avoid social situations. Consider Doreen. She is twenty-four years old, of average appearance, and works as a receptionist at the headquarters of a large hotel chain. She feels that at parties others are evaluating her looks and judging everything she says. She feels that her every move is scrutinized and found lacking. Doreen dreads any kind of social situation and particularly avoids having to meet new men. Doreen is terribly anxious and sometimes depressed.

In some cases, fear of social situations is truly phobic in nature. Some people feel intense anxiety. Autonomic responses signal danger and the fight-or-flight syndrome is activated. They feel lightheaded, their heart is racing, concentration is difficult, and palms are sweaty. They usually fear that their difficulty is obvious to others, and this adds to the distress.

Whether you are procrastinating in your social life due to depression or anxiety, it's important to push yourself to get out there and participate. Here are some suggestions.

- If you're anxious about evaluation, use cognitive restructuring to neutralize fear so that you can remain mentally present in the situation. Mind reading is the fallacy that you know what others are thinking. Before you go to a social setting, think of some phrases to say to yourself to calm your fears.

- In a group social situation, set a goal of making at least one comment every thirty minutes or so. Once you have spoken up, don't let yourself fall into negative evaluation. Reward yourself by feeling good that you took the risk—no matter what the response.

- Plan to attend social functions for short periods of time. Set a goal of staying out with others for at least an hour.

- Practice deep breathing throughout the event and do some stretching exercises before you go.

- Set a goal of attending a certain number of social events each month. If you can't schedule many, make a goal of starting a conversation with someone new each week.

- Attend a social event with a friend. Provide support and encouragement to each other.

Housework

Coming home from work or school, you may look at the basket of laundry and say, "I can't. Not tonight. Maybe tomorrow." Feeling that housework is a drudgery is not uncommon, especially for people who have many other interests and activities. Housework can also seem endless—even if you do the laundry today, it will only get dirty again. There sometimes seems to be no end to the chores you can do around a house—chipped paint to repair, dishes to wash, lawn to mow, on, and on. You may think, "Why bother starting; there's no end."

You may find it hard to believe, but some people use housework as a way of procrastinating on other tasks. Many students have told me that they use routine household chores as a way of avoiding projects like studying for exams or writing term papers. Selected jobs around the house, such as mopping the floor, have a beginning, middle, and end, all of which occur within minutes or a few hours at the most. Being able to complete a chore seems comforting when working on a difficult school project that may take months or years of diligence.

However, if you're like many people who are procrastinating on at least one household project, consider the following points for getting action.

- Get your materials for each task organized into a convenient location. You may be avoiding sewing a ripped hem or replacing a button because the thread is in one closet, the buttons in another, and you're not sure where the scissors are. Put task-related materials together—preferably in a basket for easy transport—and locate them near where you will use them.

- Get a task partner. House cleaning is easier on the psyche if you know you're not in it alone. If you are doing the dishes, one of the kids can be dusting in the next room. Or you can work on the dishes together. Company will make it easier for both of you.

- According to Stephanie Winston, author of *Getting Organized*, housework can be broken down into layers: Layer 1 consists of tasks to be done daily; Layer 2, weekly tasks; Layer 3, monthly tasks; and Layer 4 is special projects. Think of all the jobs to be done in your home and list them on the layers from 1 to 4. Once tasks are listed, designate days and times for all routine tasks (Layers 1, 2, and 3). Take these appointments as seriously as you would any work, school, or social event. Eventually you have habits in place. You'll find that you automatically stop for groceries on the way home on designated days.

- Break tasks down into small steps. Cleaning out the garage after years of neglect is a daunting experience. Don't attempt it all at once. Choose one shelf to work on. Clean it off and put back items that belong together. Don't worry about the mess you're creating. It will become a task to be tackled later. Just focus on one shelf at a time.

- The Swiss Cheese approach discussed in Chapter 7 is very effective for household chores. Poking holes in unpleasant tasks is a fairly easy way to get past them without investing a lot of time or thought. For example, you cannot clean the kitchen before you leave for work in the morning, but you can load the dishwasher in the five spare minutes before rushing out the door.

Personal Projects

All too often, last on the list of things to do are the projects you plan for yourself. The demands of work, children, family, and house always seem to be more immediate. The needs of children, of course, are important and it's hard to justify taking off for a French class if a child is sick. Somehow, though, in spite of all the competing demands, it's important to make time for yourself. It's hard to imagine that you can be as good to your work and family as you want to be if you're feeling exhausted and starved for personal fulfillment. Some books suggest that you fit your personal projects in while doing something else; for example, listening to language tapes while doing the laundry. This type of scheduling works for some people. Others find themselves feeling even more harried and dissatisfied. Here are some thoughts you should consider if you've been postponing your personal agenda:

- When you've struggled through procrastination of organizing your household routine, you'll find that you actually have more time for other activities. There is a dividend that you can use for yourself.

- Negotiate with your spouse for time for yourself. Your spouse also may have some unfulfilled needs. You can designate times when each of you can work undisturbed on his or her personal project. If you're a single parent, you may be able to negotiate a deal with a grandparent or friend. Or, if possible, hire a sitter for a few hours while you pursue your work.

- Whatever your solution, schedule a time for your personal project and, barring crises, stick to it. Make your plans now before you become so resentful of others' demands on your time that you act in a way to damage important relationships.

Procrastination and Your Child

Knowing the anxiety and self-doubt that procrastination can bring, it is particularly hard to watch someone close to you experience this pain. Mimi alternated among sadness, disappointment, fear, anger, and frustration as she saw her teenage daughter pass the time playing music videos and shopping. She was frustrated and angry that her daughter put too little effort into schoolwork even though she was very bright. She was saddened by her lack of involvement in extracurricular and social activities. She feared that her daughter was heading for a dead end.

Seeing others engage in self-destructive behavior is especially difficult when it is your child. The nature of the parent-child relationship is to be protective. You have tried for so many years to nurture and guide, it's difficult not to take the procrastination personally and to feel hurt and rejected. It's also natural to have dreams that your child will fulfill some expectations for success. When procrastination occurs you feel let down and helpless. Mimi tried to be helpful and encouraging. When her daughter did not respond, she withdrew a bit. She then tried to "tell her like it is" but again got no response. Mimi withdrew again, this time hurt and angry.

All people who procrastinate have a reason for the behavior, and to be helpful, it's necessary to first understand that reason. Understanding others' stage of change also is needed. When a child procrastinates, it is very often an act of independence. The child is announcing the right to make decisions. Unfortunately, as with all of us, some decisions are poor ones. Nevertheless, the stubborn refusal to engage in productive activity may seem to the child the loudest, clearest form of self-assertion. When rebellion is one cause of procrastination, encouraging, cajoling, and threatening will only result in further refusal to act. You will need to use subtle support instead. Try to point out the advantages of change. Find ways to make it seem like your child's idea. Don't push, but if your child begins to take action, be there with encouragement.

There may be times when your child is procrastinating not out of rebellion but out of fear. It is important to recognize when this is occurring. In this case, you may be of help in offering support and encouragement. But again, your child may reject your help. In struggling for independence, the last thing your child may want to acknowledge is the need for your help. You can only be as helpful as your child will allow you to be. It's important, though, to let your child know that you are there when needed and you're not going to be smug or judgmental.

Also try to assess your child's stage of change. If he or she is still in the precontemplation stage, your best approach is to help your child develop awareness that there is a problem. Direct confrontation will drive the child further into denial. It's best to suggest that there may be a problem, or ask if they see a problem and how you can help. If your child has progressed to the contemplation stage, you can ask how you can be supportive or just offer to help. Panic and anger on your part can only damage the relationship and reduce motivation for change. Patience is the key. If you behave in a genuinely warm, concerned way, your opinion will have much more value for others.

Procrastination and Your Spouse

In their late thirties, Walt and Ilsa have been married for two years. They recently relocated, bought a house, and now they are expecting their second child. Ilsa is feeling increasing pressure to manage all of the recent changes. Walt occasionally feels the stress but in general has a more laid-back approach to life than his wife. Ilsa always felt that Walt approached work in sporadic fits of effort. She feels Walt is getting less done lately. He always took care of the finances, but she found the bills too often unpaid, and she recently assumed this job herself. Walt has not begun work on the new baby's room and has not started to set up his consulting business to generate extra revenue. Walt senses that he is not working steadily toward his goals. He resents Ilsa's prompting and feels that she can only find fault with his efforts. Lately, caustic remarks are turning into full-blown arguments, and no one knows how to stop.

Walt and Ilsa are approaching their new responsibilities with an old plan. They are not communicating well and cannot help each other deal with the new stress in their lives. Walt could be effective but is having difficulty prioritizing work and getting started. He wonders if he is up to the demands of his new life. Ilsa is becoming increasingly anxious about their situation and tries to increase her sense of control by pushing Walt to do more. She feels that she is being harsh but doesn't know what else to do.

Procrastination in a spouse can be difficult to understand since your spouse is an adult and *should* know better. But again, as with all people who procrastinate, there are reasons for avoidance. Before you try any intervention to "help" your spouse improve productivity, first consider why procrastination is occurring. Is your spouse anxious and disorganized, or maybe exerting some control in the situation by refusing to act? You may have your opinions, but it's important to hear your spouse's thoughts on the subject too. In listening to him or her, you can also assess your spouse's level of awareness regarding the behavior. Your spouse may be unaware of procrastinating on a task and be unaware that it matters to you.

In addition to assessing your spouse's awareness of the problem and reasons for postponing, you need to get a sense of your spouse's interest in change. Understanding your spouse's stage of change will help you to cope with the present situation and know how to help. Walt is in one contemplative stage of change. He knows there is a problem and can acknowledge it. His wife can best help by showing her appreciation for his honesty and then working with him on a plan to take them through the preparation and action stage of change. Ilsa is not yet acknowledging her problem with anxiety. The focus remains on Walt and his inability to get things done. Walt too can help Ilsa by gently focusing on her problem and offering to help, and being supportive when she needs it. People in the maintenance stage of change also need supportive relationships. In the maintenance stage, relapse into old behavior patterns is a key concern. Partners need to give each other permission to be honest, to express fears, and point out pitfalls.

You also will need to decide how important it is to you that your spouse's task be done. You need to consider how procrastination affects you. Are you threatened financially by your spouse's procrastination? Is your safety or your child's threatened? When you get a sense of the importance of the job, you'll make a better decision about how to act. You also need to assess how your spouse's procrastination affects your relationship. Are you feeling resentful, disrespectful? Even if you're not harmed, do you feel that your spouse is diminishing the dreams you had together?

If you feel that your spouse's procrastination is harming your well-being or the relationship, try to talk together about your feelings. Let your spouse pick the time and place. Use feeling statements such as, "When you _____, I feel _____." Don't accuse or label your spouse's behavior. If you find yourself expressing a lot of anger, you have waited too long to have the conversation. Take a break and then resume discussing your feelings. Work to negotiate a solution to your impasse. You may use behavioral contracting to clarify expectations. The contracting process sets timelines for completion and consequences for incompletion. The next chapter, on support, covers this in more detail. Once you have negotiated your compromise, drop it. Do not make snide, sarcastic remarks on an ongoing basis, which will generate further resentment and obstinance. Be encouraging. Be sure to notice and compliment small steps toward the goal.

It is important not to judge your spouse for procrastinating. Labeling a person by one or just a few characteristics is inaccurate and damaging. Your spouse has many qualities—some good, some not so perfect. Keep sight of these better qualities and let your spouse know you appreciate him or her.

12

Support

Some people who procrastinate are loathe to ask for support. They feel embarrassed about their difficulty in getting things done and go to great lengths to cover up this performance problem. Self-consciousness is closely associated with the problem of procrastination. Embarrassment often takes the form of defensiveness, and the thought of asking for support seems the final disgrace. Many who procrastinate feel that asking for support is a private admission of weakness and a public statement of imperfection. They fear that such a public admission will open the door to critical evaluation and further self-doubt.

Getting support does not have to be an emotionally risky endeavor. We accept the athlete who needs the help of teammates, and we expect a student to need occasional guidance. In many professions, especially medicine, consultation from others is routine. When support is defined as providing a positive influence for others, it's easy to see that everyone needs it. Support you find from others should be focused on the task, and it should feel good to receive it. Support is never critical, judgmental, or embarrassing. Remember also that you are maintaining personal control by asking for support. In deciding that you are stuck and want to move on, you have initiated action. You have extended the invitation to others, and you are still free to limit the input at any time.

When receiving support, guard against letting others come to your rescue. You may consciously, or not, want to escape the struggle of getting things done. Others may consciously, or not, want to take control for you. Rescue is, of course, not support. It ultimately does not feel good. You will be left with the feeling of self-doubt and fear of taking on new challenges necessary for your further development.

Support has many forms. You may find all the help you need in discussing your problem with a close friend. Other forms of support include finding a task partner, writing contracts, joining groups, or getting professional help. This chapter will outline each type of support. Think of the task you have chosen to work on throughout this book. Consider each type of support in relationship to your task and how it would help you to get the job done.

Feedback

The simplest form of support is talking over your situation with someone else. Talking to others seems to help clarify thoughts. You find that you have questions and concerns of which you were only vaguely aware. You also find that you have ideas and solutions previously unknown to you.

The quality of the support you receive will depend on the person(s) you choose for help. Close friends, of course, can provide some excellent advice since they know your tendency to procrastinate and are used to seeing through your excuses. However, good friends do have their biases, and you need to assess whether you're getting thoughtful words applying to your situation or just deeply held personal beliefs. At work, you may have a friend to turn to. If not, consider discussing your procrastination problem with someone outside of the work environment. An outsider can give you an independent opinion and maintain your privacy—sparing your personal problems from becoming part of office politics.

People often want to know if it's best to discuss their problem with someone who has had the same experience. You really don't need to reject someone as a confidant because of differing experiences. You want to find someone who is rational and a good listener. In fact, it can be a good idea to talk with someone who has had very different experiences from you. You may learn a whole new approach to your problem and get a fresh perspective on the task. Regardless of the person's experience or position, you do not have to take the advice offered. You are taking control of your problem by asking for input and you maintain control by deciding for yourself what directives, if any, you will take.

When seeking advice, be sure to ask specific questions. Your goal is to get help for thinking through your difficulty with this task. You'll get more helpful advice if you focus the discussion specifically on what you need to know. If you are in the precontemplation stage of change, ask others to help you identify your defenses. You might begin by saying, "How did you think I reacted when...?" Your reaction to feedback also is important. If you respond by getting angry or making excuses, you will inhibit honest discussion. You also reduce the likelihood of getting advice in the future. Also be specific in the kind of support you want from others. If you are in the preparation stage of change, let people know your plan. Let them know too what you want them to do to help and what you would like them not to do or say as you get started with your change program.

Task Partner·

Another level of support involves finding a partner for your task. A task partner can provide all of the benefits of simple feedback. A partner can be very helpful in the beginning of the action stage of change. Finding someone who understands and advises you in your work is the first step in determining a partner for the job. Once you agree to work with someone, you then have the added benefit of companionship. Having a partner can reduce the sense of being overwhelmed and alone in your work.

There are a few different ways to work with a partner. You may exchange plans and monitor each other's progress. This technique has been tremendously effective in helping students to keep up with required studying. In one experiment, students met and quizzed each other on study progress one or two times per week.

In combination with other techniques, such as a To Do list and scheduling, students found working with a partner to be highly effective in increasing course work.

Other partnership arrangements involve enlisting help in actually performing the job. You can, for example, offer to help paint your neighbor's garage in exchange for some help with your yard work. Working jointly with someone seems to increase productivity since you want to avoid the disappointment of your partner more than you want to avoid the unpleasantness of the task. Finally, just having someone present while you do your work can be comforting. A student in my class on overcoming procrastination decided to ask a friend over while she studied for the bar exam. The friend filled out applications to graduate school. Together, the two of them made progress on an avoided task and took comfort in knowing they weren't alone in pushing themselves through a dreaded job.

Contracts

One way to formalize your working arrangement with a partner is to develop a contract. A contract can be a simple verbal agreement between two or more people. More often, though, contracts are written. By writing your agreement, the promise becomes formal and important. The idea of contracting may seem a bit stiff at first, but once you've tried it, you may find that it's a simple way of making expectations clear and increasing your effectiveness. Contracts between people are often a good idea when the job is likely to take a long time to complete or the work involved is very difficult. Lengthy, hard work creates conditions under which behavior often breaks down and progress stops. With a contract, you and your partner are more likely to keep going to complete your own part of the bargain.

An effective contract will include a few key points. First, it is important to be specific about the work you and your partner will complete. Stating that you will help your son fix his bike in exchange for help with household chores is vague and subject to misinterpretation. A better statement would be that you will help your son fix the flat tire on his bike on Saturday from one to three in the afternoon in exchange for making his bed on a daily basis and taking out the trash on Wednesday. Contracts also should state consequences for successful and unsuccessful completion. You can cancel rewards, such as going out for ice cream after both tasks are done, or you can specify make-up work that must be completed before any reciprocal work will be done. Finally, be clear on dates when the work is due. A contract between father and son for household chores in exchange for help with the bike might look like this:

Contract

I, Nate, agree to make my bed every day by 7:30 a.m. and to take out the trash on Wednesday by 7:00 p.m.

I, Dad, agree to help Nate fix the flat tire on his bike on Saturday between 1:00 and 3:00 p.m.

Consequences:

If I, Nate, do not complete my work by times scheduled, Dad will not help fix the flat tire on Saturday.

If I, Dad, do not help Nate with the flat tire on Saturday, I will give Nate money to have the flat tire repaired at the local garage.

_____   _____
Nate's signature   Dad's signature

_____   _____
Date   Date

In the maintenance stage of change, you may want to continue using a contract, but the terms can be modified to reflect a different need. The contract should specify terms when slipups occur—what the consequences will be; how your partner will respond.

Self-Help Groups

Self-help groups have a long and successful history helping people to change bad habits. Alcoholics Anonymous has helped millions of people to stop drinking. Borrowing on its success, groups of all kinds have sprung up to help people quit drugs and smoking, to alter bad eating habits, and to manage money responsibly. There is no research that tells us exactly why these groups are so helpful to people in reducing long-standing, difficult behavior problems. One common element, though, is the validation of each person in the group. When you are struggling to manage self-defeating behavior, you can feel very alone and depleted. In a group setting, surrounded by others who share your problem, you feel a sense of relief. In teaching my course on overcoming procrastination, I am struck by the consistent remarks about the relief of finding others in the same situation. Once students do not have to direct their energy toward defending themselves for having the problem of procrastination, they freely turn to much more goal-directed behavior. In addition to social acceptance by the group, you may find that you can contribute ideas to others about how to more effectively approach an avoided task. Approaches that have failed for others are valuable lessons too.

If there is not a class or group on managing procrastination available to you, consider forming your own. There are a number of important points to be incorporated into effective group experience:

- If no one in the group has experience leading group discussions, recruit someone who does. The effectiveness of the group depends on providing support to others. Criticism, teasing, or disinterest cannot be allowed. Someone needs to be responsible for maintaining a helpful approach.

- Group size should not exceed six to eight members. A group larger than eight does not afford each member a personal experience and limits the time and detail that each member's issues can receive.

- Set ground rules for group dynamics. Make it clear that the purpose of the group is to provide support for the members. Members should know that only encouragement and constructive ideas are to be shared.

- Members should be aware of the stages of change. Efforts to support others should match the current stage. Pushing others to action will only demotivate and disrupt the group.

- Meet at a standard time and in a designated location. It's best not to plan to meet over lunch or in other settings that can be distracting to the group's purpose.

- Try to focus discussions on a specific task for a member. General discussions of how difficult it is to get things done do not leave anyone with a sense of accomplishment.

- Establish informal time limits on each member's turn to speak. When discussing problems with task completion, members should be brief and talk specifically about the task at hand. If a member expresses real depression and isn't functioning well in most aspects of life, the self-help group is not the appropriate setting; he or she may need professional help.

- Determine at the first session how many weeks you will meet. Eight to ten are recommended to address the specific problem of assisting each other to begin or to complete a task.

Professional Help

There are times when talking to a friend, finding a partner, signing a contract, or joining a group is not enough. If you have tried to change and cannot, or you cannot maintain the change, enlisting professional support may be a good idea. You may be having difficulty understanding or implementing self-change procedures. Help from a professional source can be useful. Another consideration in deciding to seek professional help is the importance of the problem to you. If you are suffering and paying a high price for your procrastination, it makes sense to seek relief from a competent professional.

As you know, procrastination is often a feature of depression. Depression is a common emotional problem. Studies indicate that 11 million people, or 6 percent of the adult population, will experience an episode of depression each year. Depression is treatable with both behavior therapy and medication. If you have lost interest in your usual activities for two weeks, you should seek competent professional help.

Anxiety is another emotional problem that can be serious enough to warrant professional help. Some people are so anxious that they are considered to be phobic. Social phobias—fear of social contact—can be debilitating. If you feel that despite your best efforts, you continue to avoid situations, particularly those involving people and the possibility of evaluation, you can be helped by a trained therapist.

Treatment today tends to be short term and problem focused. You need not fear that you will spend years on the analyst's couch contemplating your childhood. You may work with a therapist for a few sessions on managing anxiety or reducing depression. You may choose to see a therapist for professional guidance on reducing and then managing procrastination. If you are not making progress on your own and feel that continuing to procrastinate will cost you dearly in terms of your personal or professional life, you should seek help.

To find a therapist, a recommendation from a friend is the best place to start. A therapist who worked successfully with a friend has some likelihood of succeeding with you. Also you can discuss the therapist's approach with your friend and make a more informed choice. When meeting with your therapist, ask a lot of questions at the outset. There are many approaches to therapy and you want to choose one that will work for you. Ask the therapist what approach to your problem will be used and decide if you are comfortable with it. Plan with your therapist what problems you will address, how many sessions you will meet, and what outcomes can be expected. Also discuss the payment plan. Most health insurance programs will pay part of the cost of therapy. Procrastination though is not at present a recognized psychiatric disorder and some insurance programs will not reimburse for its treatment. Related problems such as anxiety and depression though are covered. If you must assume some or all of the cost of treatment, find out about a "sliding scale" fee which is payment based on income. You can also discuss setting up a payment plan to cover the costs of the treatment.

Even if you choose to work with a therapist on procrastination or related issues, you will ultimately determine your own success. A therapist cannot solve problems for you or anyone else. A therapist can guide, advise, and encourage, but only you can do the work that will result in change.

Choosing your method of support from others will be a cornerstone of your work on overcoming procrastination. It is as valid and important as task-directed thinking and effectively organizing your work environment. Some approaches may feel awkward at first, but if you've chosen your support well, you will benefit enormously from the advice and encouragement.

Exercise

Consider the task you have chosen to work on throughout this book. Choose a support technique appropriate for you and your task. Write your choice on the Task Work Sheet.

13

Final Points

In the course of reading this book, you have learned about the relationship between procrastination and anxiety, depression, and low-conscientiousness. You have thought about your own experiences and analyzed your motivation for putting things off. You also have discovered your excuses for procrastinating, noting whether you are blaming others, you are addicted to being busy, or the like. Finally, you have thought through many techniques to get things done and selected those that seem right for you. Now it's time to act.

While you have been experimenting along the way with some new ideas and approaches, your plan is only now complete and can be fully implemented. You will be leaving the preparation stage of change and moving to the action stage. There are a number of points that will help you to persist in your efforts and, finally, to change.

Be Realistic

Once you have completed your plan, you may expect all your problems with getting things done to resolve easily. This is especially true if you have a problem with conscientiousness and get frustrated easily. Real change takes time. There are a lot of adjustments to be made. Not only do you need to get comfortable with a new way of working, but others will need to adjust to your new sense of purposefulness. Prepare yourself to go slowly, adjust to each change, analyze any obstacles, and then to move on.

Use What Works

Learning to overcome procrastination requires experimentation. You will initially choose techniques that appeal to you. Your hunches will most often be right. There may be times, though, when your plan isn't working. This can occur if you are applying an old plan to a new problem or if circumstances have changed substantially for you or your task. Maintain the flexibility to change parts of your plan as needed. Guard against using the same techniques over and over if they are not leaving you feeling satisfied with your effort. Try new techniques or combinations of techniques until you hit on the right formula for you.

Own It

It's worth remembering that it's *your* procrastination. No one can change it for you. Change can be difficult and you may be tempted to run away from it. Or you may struggle with part of your problem, such as denial. For example, you may deny that you feel anxious or depressed. A lot of effort can go into maintaining these facades. You will not be able to completely resolve your problem with procrastination until you face it in its entirety. You can work through your denial like any other obstacle to progress by using the techniques outlined in this book. You will typically need to listen to feedback from friends and colleagues to get you started in recognizing and facing denial.

While not really denying that a problem exists, you may experience resistance to moving ahead with your plan. It's important to acknowledge this resistance. Resistance may be telling you that your plan is incomplete because you have missed some important part of your motivation for procrastination. Or your resistance may tell you that you are not really invested in this task at all and you would be better off placing your efforts elsewhere. Whatever the source of resistance, it is to be analyzed and resolved as any other problem encountered in accomplishing your goal.

Relapse

Prochaska and colleagues have studied relapses extensively. They prefer to call this stage "recycling." Setbacks are recognized as a standard part of the change process. Prochaska reports that only about 20 percent of people are able to change their behavior on the first try. Most people should expect and prepare for setbacks. Relapse is most often caused by emotional stress. When emotions get out of order, it is common to revert to old, more comfortable ways of behaving. Many times people excuse their behavior by saying that, for example, they deserve to smoke—after all, they just lost a job or a loved one. Besides emotional turmoil, lapses in environmental management contribute most often to setbacks. This means, for example, if you have finally been able to get control of your spending habits, you may begin to let yourself carry credit cards again. Then any small emotional distress occurs and you are set up to slip back into old spending habits.

The opposite of excusing one small indiscretion is to overreact to one small slip. If you do momentarily relapse and give in to temptation, this doesn't necessarily mean you've failed. Try to see one indiscretion as just that. Get back on the program and try again.

The difficulty with relapse is the negative emotions that are generated. Feelings of failure, discouragement, demoralization can

---

Exercise

With your plan in place and realistic expectations for progress, you are now ready to move on to the next stage of change. Review your work sheet. Be sure you have filled it out completely. As your last step in the plan, set a date for review and revision. Place that date on your Task Work Sheet and you're ready to begin.

occur. If they do, you can be dragged into a second problem—combating negative emotions that make it all the more difficult to think clearly and direct your behavior back to action.

When relapse occurs, complete failure is rarely the result. It isn't likely that you will need to start over from the beginning in your plan for change. You may just slip back to the contemplation stage. You can then prepare a revised plan and move into action again. It is important to extract the benefits of relapse. Learn why you slipped. Then, be conscious of these pitfalls. You can profitably build prevention into your next plan for change.

References

Alberti, R. and Emmons, M. (1974). *Your Perfect Right*. San Luis Obispo, CA: Impact Press.

Bailey, C. (1991). *The New Fit or Fat*. Boston: Houghton Mifflin.

Beck, A. T. (1979). *Cognitive Therapy and Emotional Disorders*. New York: New American Library.

Beswick, G., Rothblum, E.; and Mann, L. (1988). *Psychological Antecedents of Student Procrastination*. (Vol. 23).

Blatt, S. J. and Quinlan, P. (1967). Punctual and Procrastinating Students: A Study of Temporal Parameters. *Journal of Consulting Psychology, 31*, 169–174.

Boice, R. (1989). Procrastination, Busyness and Bingeing. *Behavior Research and Therapy, 27*, 605–611.

Burka, J. B. and Yuen, L. M. (1983). *Procrastination: Why You Do It and What to Do About It*. Reading, MA: Addison-Wesley.

Burns, D. D. (1980). *Feeling Good: The New Mood Therapy*. New York: Signet.

Ellis, A. and Harper, R. A. (1975). *A New Guide to Rational Living*. Hollywood: Wilshire Book Co.

Ellis, A. and Knaus, W. J. (1977). *Overcoming Procrastination*. New York: Signet.

Ferrari, J. (1991). Compulsive Procrastination: Some Self-Reported Characteristics. *Psychological Reports, 68,* 455–458.

Ferrari, J. and Olivette, M. J. (1993). Perceptions of Parental Control and the Development of Indecision Among Late Adolescent Females. *Adolescence, 28,* 963–970.

Ferrari, J. (1992). Procrastinators and Perfect Behavior: An Exploratory Factor Analysis of Self-Presentation, Self-Awareness, and Self-Handicapping Components. *Journal of Research in Personality, 26,* 75–84.

Ferrari, J., Johnson, J., and McGown, W. (1995). *Procrastination and Task Avoidance: Theory, Research, and Treatment.* New York: Plenum.

Flett, G. L., Blankstein, K. R., and Hewitt, P. L. (1992). Components of Perfectionism and Procrastination in College Students. *Journal of Behavior and Personality, 20,* 85–94.

Flett, G. L., Hewitt, P. L., and Mikail, S. (1993). Dimensions of Perfectionism in Marital Distress. Paper presented at the annual meeting of American Psychological Associates, Toronto.

Green, L. (1982). Minority Students' Self-Control of Procrastination. *Journal of Counseling Psychology, 29,* 636–644.

Harris, M. B. and Trujillo, A. E. (1975). Improving Study Habits of Junior High School Students Through Self-Management Versus Group Discussion. *Journal of Counseling Psychology, 23,* 513–517.

Harris, N. H. and Sutton, R. I. (1983). Task Procrastination in Organizations: A Framework for Research. *Human Relations, 36,* 987–996.

Hill, M. B., Hill, D. A., Chabot, A. E., and Barrall, J. F. (1978). A Survey of College Faculty and Student Procrastination. *College Student Journal, 12,* 256–262.

Knaus, W. (1979). *Do It Now: How to Stop Procrastinating.* Englewood Cliffs, NJ: Prentice-Hall.

Lakein, A. (1973). *How To Get Control of Your Time and Your Life.* New York: Signet.

Lay, C. H. (1986). At Last, My Research Article on Procrastination. *Journal of Research in Personality, 20,* 474–495.

Lay, C. H. (1987). A Modal Profile Analysis of Procrastinators: A Search for Types. *Personality and Individual Differences, 8,* 705–714.

Lay, C. H. (1988). The Relationship of Procrastination and Optimism to Judgements of Time to Complete an Essay and Anticipation of Setbacks. *Journal of Social Behavior and Personality, 3,* 201–214.

Lay, C. H., Knish, S., and Zanatta, R. (1992). Self-Handicappers and Procrastinators: A Comparison of Their Practice Behavior Prior to an Evaluation. *Journal of Research in Personality, 26,* 242–257.

Lay, C. H. and Schouwenburg, H. C. (1993). Trait Procrastination, Time Management, and Academic Behavior. *Journal of Social Behavior and Personality, 8,* 647–662.

Lindsley, D. B. (1951). Emotion. In S. S. Stevens (Ed.), *Handbook of Experimental Psychology.* New York: Wiley.

McGown, W., Petzel, T., and Rupert, P. (1987). Personality Correlates and Behaviors of Chronic Procrastinators. *Personality and Individual Differences, 11,* 71–79.

McGown, W. & Roberts, R. (1994). Studies of Academic and Work-related Dysfunctioning Relevant to the College Version of Indirect Measure of Impulsive Behavior. In *Integra Technical Paper.* Radnor, PA: Integra, Inc.

McGown, W. G. and Johnson, J. L. (1989). Nonstudent Validation of an Adult Inventory of Procrastination. Paper presented at the American Psychological Association, New Orleans.

McKay, M., Rogers, P. D., and McKay, J. (1989). *When Anger Hurts: Quieting the Storm Within.* Oakland, CA: New Harbinger Publications.

Milgram, N. A., Sroloff, B., and Rosenbaum, M. (1988). The Procrastination of Everyday Life. *Journal of Research, 22,* 197–212.

Prochaska, J. O., Norcross, J. C., and DiClemente, C. C. (1994). *Changing for Good.* New York: William Morrow.

Rothblum, E. D. (1990). Fear of Failure: The Psychodynamic Need Achievement, Fear of Success, and Procrastination Models. In H. Leitenberg (Ed.), *Handbook of Social and Evaluation Anxiety,* 497–537. New York: Plenum.

Rothblum, E. D., Solomon, L. J., and Murakami, J. (1986). Affective, Cognitive, and Behavioral Differences Between High and Low Procrastinators. *Journal of Counseling Psychology, 33,* 387–394.

Scharf, D. and Hait, P. (1985). *Studying Smart.* New York: Harper & Row.

Schecter, C., Vanchieri, C. F., and Crofton, C. (1990). Evaluating Women's Attitudes and Perceptions in Developing Mammography Promotion Messages. *Public Health Reports, 3,* 253–257.

Schouwenburg, H. C. (1992). Procrastinators and Fear of Failure: An Exploration of Reasons for Procrastination. *European Journal of Personality, 6,* 225–236.

Smith, M. (1975). *When I Say No I Feel Guilty.* New York: The Dial Press.

Solomon, L. J. and Rothblum, E. D. (1984). Academic Procrastination: Frequency and Cognitive-Behavioral Correlates. *Journal of Counseling Psychology, 31,* 503–509.

Sommer, W. G. (1990). Procrastination and Cramming: How Adept Students Ace the System. *Journal of Academic and College Health, 39,* 5–10.

Taylor, R. (1979). *Procrastination: The Personality and Situational Correlates of Procrastination Behavior for Achievement Tasks.* Unpublished Dissertation, Dissertation Abstracts International.

Widseth, J. C. (1987). Hearing the Theme of Archaic Grandiosity in Procrastination by College Students. *Journal of College Student Psychotherapy, 1,* 91–98.

Winston, S. (1978). *Getting Organized.* New York: Warner Books.

Wolpe, J. (1973). *The Practice of Behavior Therapy.* Elmsford, NY: Pergamon Press.

Ziesat, H. A., Rosenthal, T. L., and White, G. M. (1978). Behavioral Self-Control in Treating Procrastination of Studying. *Psychological Reports, 42,* 59–69.